BOATOWNER'S LEGAL GUIDE

BOATOWNER'S LEGAL GUIDE

WILLIAM P. CRAWFORD

Library of Congress Catalog Card No: 74-33189
ISBN 0-87799-050-6

Designed by Randall DeLeeuw

A Sea/Haessner Nautical Book;
published by arrangement with
CBS Publications.
Haessner Publishing, Inc.
Newfoundland, New Jersey 07435

Printed in the United States of America

6 Boatowner's

CONTENTS

SECTION 1

There is, perhaps, no more wonderful discovery than the delights of pleasure boating. Whether your leisure time is spent at the wheel of an 18-foot trailerboat or, cap atilt, aboard a sleek cruiser, the thrills of adventure and command are the same. Big or small, sail or power. . . this is your ship, and you are her captain.

The purpose of this book is to help you keep the pleasure in your pleasure boating. For nothing can spoil the fun faster than a troublesome legal snarl in ownership or operation. Pleasure boating without some knowledge of the legal factors involved is no more practical than football without rules. Moreover, there is an extra measure of enjoyment in recognizing even the broad outlines of the colorful patterns of boating law.

Stand by, then, to cast off on a tour of the misty seas of Admiralty law. At the helm, directing our progress, will be experts in law, insurance, finance, brokerage and government regulations. For this review was prepared in association with a panel of professionals. And with their help we will gain a commonsense survey of boating law.

First, a look at the Sailing Orders to learn what lies ahead. The rules of football might fit in a slim pamphlet; but we can expect no such simplicity here. Neither a single volume, nor a shelf-full, can possibly contain our mammoth subject. Just as futile is a repetition of technically worded regulations. In fact, that approach can be outright deception. The normal reaction after reading an official statement of law is to wonder, "Now, just what was that all about?" After suffering through cross-references from Title X to Paragraph Y via Sub-Chapter Z, the reader still must take into account how judges will view what the lawmakers seem to have said.

We are not going to chart every ripple and eddy along the track; and that is only sensible. For, compared to football, the rules of boating law are quite subtle. Yet the intelligent boatman must still recognize its general outlines. Only then can he select safe courses of conduct and be able to judge when professional assistance might be desirable. What we are after is an overview of the area and then a practical discussion, guided by experts, of the major points along the way.

Our topics include agreements to buy, build and repair a boat, the story on liability for injuries and damage and what's in store when a crime might be committed aboard. Answers to questions in those areas would come from a conference with an attorney. To learn what a marine insurance policy is all about, a boatowner would like to meet with an insurance expert. A session with a banker would take care of questions about financing. To sit down with a customhouse broker would clear up what is involved when taking a foreign cruise or seeking to document the boat. And a meeting with government officials would reveal the patterns of regulations fashioned to control pleasure boat operation.

No book can whisk the reader personally from one such office to another; but we've done the next best thing. The chapters to follow are summaries of notes which you might take if, in fact, you had completed such a round of appointments. We would probably all ask the same key questions as we met with each expert. The answers to them, as well as to other questions prompted by discussion, lie ahead.

Introductions are now in order. In Section 2, our conference with an attorney, we are guided by Mr. James H. Ackerman. In his offices, he led us through the reefs and channels of a comprehensive legal review. Our pilot through the fascinating regions of marine insurance is Mr. Gerald Sullivan, an insurance executive. Mr. Theodore Rosata, a banking executive of long experience, directs our course during Section 4's discussion of boat financing. Charting the passage of Section 5 is Mr. Howard Hartry and his staff of customhouse brokers. And the section on government regulations was prepared after discussion with Coast Guard officers of the 11th Coast Guard District. The cooperation of Admiral James W. Williams, USCG, Ret. and his District staff is gratefully acknowledged.

Now to set the stage for our panel by a brief glance at the background of present-day boating law. The normal pace at which law develops was more or less caught napping by the upsurge in recreational boating. The result was that for a while, pleasure boatmen were totally under legal rules fashioned to serve quite a different world.

Admiralty, the title assigned to that unusual body of law, is rooted more deeply in the past than any other branch of the legal field. By nature its character is international; and much of it is related to commerce. For it was developed to serve the requirements of those who carried on trade by sea.

A new group of interests with new requirements are involved in pleasure boating. And with remarkable speed those concerned have begun to evolve new rules and standards designed for their needs. Today's boatman can already enjoy a legal climate more suitable to his purpose in taking to the sea.

The new patterns, though, are not yet complete. They don't cover all geographical areas; and where they do apply, they leave gaps. In such cases, the ancient law of Admiralty can glimmer through. For historically, whether a vessel was used for pleasure or profit, the same legal rules were in force. And because of those gaps in the cloak of modern boating law, we should first discuss what lies beneath. We're not about, of course, to get mired in deep theory or anything like it. Rather, our focus will be on one feature only: the distinctive character given a vessel in Admiralty law. By doing so we can sufficiently catch the theme of Admiralty to recognize more fully what our expert panel will later have to say. So, settle back for a few pages while we walk around backstage.

The need for standardized rules to govern business by sea was seen thousands of years ago. On one hand, the shipowner desired predictable justice wherever his ship might be. On the other, those who dealt with his ship needed workable means to settle disputes. Not all arguments were expected to end up before a judge. But the pattern, at least, had to be such that, if carried through to court, it would bring a uniform and enforceable outcome.

Now, basic to every legal hearing is that it should not be one-sided. When a judge reaches his decision, he should do so only after each side has had a chance to state his case. When the parties involved are nearby, this is readily achieved. Each can be officially notified of what is going on by service of process. But ages ago, when the first Phoenician dispatched his ship from the eastern Mediterranean to a foreign shore, the game rules had to change. He needed assurance that no "hometown" decision in an alien land would damage his interests. Even more important, a merchant who did business with the ship in that alien land required some means to hale the owner or his vessel before a judge.

How to arrange all this was the problem. In fairness, the foreign merchant should not be forced to sail the length of the Mediterranean to serve process on the Phoenician shipowner. Even the shipowner wouldn't want that; for if merchants had no nearby court, they might do no business at all with ships from distant lands.

The answer to this basic problem was developed by the businessmen themselves . . . just as the answers to present-day needs of pleasure boating are urged by those most affected. Workable rules were adopted in shipping centers; and by experience, both shipowner and merchant gained assurance that the rules would be followed. The Rhodians of the Middle East are supposed to have established such a code about 3000 years ago. Eleanor of Aquitaine, mother of King Richard the Lion-Hearted, is given credit for another, called the **Laws of Oleron.** And the **Laws of Wisbuy** were those used by courts in the Baltic to arbitrate maritime disputes.

All this is ancient history, but not quite. For the general theme still persists. In order to meet the problem of dispensing justice to distant parties, the vessel itself is given a legal personality. She can be sued; and a binding judgment can be decided against her. A ship is not just a piece of property belonging to an owner. Her status is very different to that of an automobile or a set of golf clubs. She, herself, can be held accountable for damages she inflicts or for goods and services to supply her needs. She is a "she" and not an "it". And this unique character is the key to much of the law of boating. It stems directly from the age-old principle that the owner of a vessel agrees she stand good for claims made against her wherever she might be.

Special courts have been established by maritime nations to exercise this unusual power over things as well as people. In the United States, they are the Federal District Courts, sitting in Admiralty. And the claim is called a **libel** When such a matter is filed, it is said to be a **libel in rem**; that is, against the thing itself as distinguished from its owner. Of course, the owner may also be sued; and then the libel against him is **in personam.** Claimants still retain the right to use more conventional courts to bring the owner to task. So they can bring suit against him in an appropriate city, county or state court or they can file action in the same Federal District Court not sitting in Admiralty. But only Admiralty courts are given this special power over the ship herself as a litigant.

As part of this approach, the law of Admiralty grants to claimants a very powerful legal weapon: the **maritime lien.** Basically, he who does certain business with a ship receives a sort of interest in her as security for his claim. When he brings suit against the vessel **in rem** he is enforcing his claim to that lien. And before we proceed another ship's length, we'd better find out what kind of legal billy-club it is.

In the first place, the lien is secret. It need not be recorded at any particular place; and we could hardly expect otherwise. Recordation in a port foreign to the ship might not be adequate notice to the shipowner. Yet the burden of recording it at the ship's home port, (the other end of the Mediterranean, for example), would be unfair to the claimant. Nor does the maritime lien depend on possession. A hotel might have a lien on the baggage of a guest who skips down the fire escape; but to enforce it, the hotel must usually hold on to the suitcases. A garage can have a lien on an automobile for the value of repair work done; but to enforce it, the mechanic usually must keep the car in his shop. For the ship, though, the story is different. Services are rendered to her so she may continue her labors. To make her a hostage for payment is to defeat the purpose. The result would parallel the vicious circle of the old debtor's prison: a captive debtor cannot work to pay the debt, yet until the debt is paid, he is held captive. To be workable, the maritime lien must be free of too many formal restrictions.

Now we are back full circle. The procedure to enforce that potent remedy must be predictable, uniform and certain. So the power to do so is vested in special courts which apply law tending to be internationally uniform. When a vessel is arrested by a **libel in rem**, the Admiralty court proclaims to the world that she is held subject to its power. All persons having any claim of interest in her, whether as owner or otherwise, are on notice to come forward and present their claims. The owner has a chance to free her by posting a satisfactory bond. If, though, he doesn't do so, then she stays bound to the court. The validity of claims is next judged, and they are ranked for priority of payment. If her owner does not take care of valid claims, then the vessel is auctioned off by the court to pay them.

At such a sale, the purchaser receives a clear title, unencumbered by liens or claims whether they have been presented or not. In effect the vessel is reborn. Creditors are diverted to the purchase price as a fund for payment. And should they not receive full measure, they can still sue the owner in person. But the ship is released from her obligations. She opens a new set of account books with no liabilities.

We've read enough to gain a hint of the pattern. A vessel operates in a special field of law where special circumstances require special rules. And the reasons behind the rules make good sense in the light of world commerce. More and more, today's rules of boating law steer a different course. But, as we've already noted, that new direction is not yet completely defined. And when it falters, the old-time authority of Admiralty can bark out orders.

Hereafter, as we meet the advice of experts on specific and practical topics, let's keep this introduction in mind. At the moment, the United States boating law pattern is still somewhat like Joseph's coat of many colors. In some areas, where the business of building, serving and financing small craft has been long established, the old Admiralty legal routines are quite familiar. In others, the boom of recreational boating has attracted those more in tune with shoreside law. Not surprising, then, is the discovery of geographic unevenness. And not at all possible is a "Yes" or "No" answer to many of the questions. Emerging is a national pattern to compare in uniformity and certainty with the procedures in use for motor vehicles. Again, though, the job is not complete. When Admiralty shows through, accept it as a fair, workable and efficient pattern. It is just different. Appreciation of its fundamental difference from legal matters ashore should bring with it a better grasp of prudence afloat.

SECTION 2

For the better part of a day you have been, notebook in hand, across the desk from an attorney, jotting down his comments on boating law. Well, even if that isn't exactly true, you were there by proxy. And this chapter recaps what notes you might have made. Things legal are not often suited to neat division into separate categories, so we should expect some measure of overlap between this and other chapters. In some instances, what is said elsewhere might, perhaps, have been discussed here; for an attorney is knowledgeable in many areas. But there are some topics on which we particularly look to him for comment; and our meeting with him was steered in such directions. Here, then, is what he had to say.

First off, there is the subject of *buying a boat*. For most of us, this is a big deal. We reflect carefully on our likes and dislikes, weigh the pros and cons of various features. . .and we enjoy every moment of the experience. Interest, though, sometimes falters when it comes time to close the deal. After all, just some dull paper work stands between us and adventure. But don't go off watch yet! For no matter how drab the details might appear, they require attention.

The key questions can probably be reduced to three. (1) has the seller the power to sell? (2) can he sell free and clear? and (3) has he told you all he should about the boat? The care you use to find answers will vary, of course, with the circumstances of the transaction; and the approach is about the same as that for the purchase of a carpetsweeper instead of a cruiser. You might react one way if the price is reasonable; you should be extra-alert if the price is unusually low. A reputable seller may bring one response, while one with creditors close aboard brings another. Purchase from a dealer or through a licensed broker obviously adds to confidence. Yet, always, familiarity with snares and booby traps is important.

New boating laws have greatly simplified things in some areas. Often when new law is under construction, one state serves as a proving ground, while others observe to see how these work out. California seems to be a test track for modern laws of boating. There, procedures have been set up to monitor boat sales and purchase loans. The general idea parallels that already in use for motor vehicles. Ownership is shown by a certificate issued by a state agency. When a boat is not paid for in full, the creditor can appear of record as legal owner. Regulation of that sort greatly simplifies an investigation of title. But such a pattern may not apply in your area; so it is essential to learn what procedures your state affords for recording title and transfers. An efficient way to learn the name of the proper agency is to call the local office of the tax assessor; for often such state procedures are tied in with tax collection routines. Should there exist procedures in your state, you can learn from the proper agency what form of documents might be specified, what steps are required...and details of the boat's history will surely come to light.

Such patterns, though, are not at all universal. Nor need they be the exclusive ones used in the state where they are in force. Not every boat need be under such a plan. An example is a *documented vessel.* When a boat is of 5 net tons or more, its title and legal history might be represented by a document issued by the U.S. Coast Guard. Later on we will spend a chapter with a Customs Broker and find out more of this. For now, we should just note that title records might exist at the *Office of Marine Inspection for the Coast Guard District* of the boat's home port. An inquiry there could be worthwhile.

Should a vessel be *bought from a foreign source,* the added problems of customs import duties and, perhaps, paperwork with a foreign consulate, can arise. An experienced broker or attorney can be of great aid in such a transaction. Incidentally, it might be well to note in passing that the *sale* of a U.S. vessel to an alien can involve the permit of the Maritime Administration, U.S. Department of Commerce. When that kind of business is pending, attorneys and brokers will usually be on the scene; but it is well to appreciate that such a complication can develop.

What about the piece of paper which represents the transfer of title? What about the *Bill of Sale*?[1] First of all, it should exist. Buying a boat by conversation and a handclasp might sometimes be possible; but it is also absurd. The content of the paper is often shaped by official regulations. And always it should be expected to say no more than the words on its face. There are important exceptions to this last statement; for the seller can be held to some unspoken or *implied warranties.* But an effective way to avoid mix-up is to have things expressed clearly. Of course, when law requires a particular form to be used, then it should be followed. The combination of such a paper and the procedures specified for its execution and recording can take care of the problem.

But when there is no established routine in use, the buyer should have in mind some basic points. He should expect the seller to say in writing that he is the owner and has the power to sell, that he does sell and that he accepts the price. The seller should also either state that there are no claims against the boat, or else list what ones are outstanding. Safest is to

[1] *See page 85*

have a lawyer draw such a Bill of Sale. Certainly, since a cruiser isn't a carpetsweeper, the transaction justifies such protection.

To gain the seller's assurance that *title is clear* and that no liens exist is a firm base for suit against him should, in fact, a problem arise. Far better though, is assurance beforehand that the problem won't develop. Modern boating laws provide some protection on that score when the vessel is registered and operating in a particular state. New requirements, as in force in California, can spotlight such trouble as unclear title and unpaid loans. In time, the application of general Admiralty law with its powerful maritime lien will possibly contract to the area of commercial vessels. Already, its impact on pleasure craft in some areas seems limited to large yachts. For Admiralty remedies are costly and time-consuming. But the potential is still there. Good judgment will dictate when concern for maritime liens is a significant danger.

In order to make the use of an Admiralty court worthwhile, the stakes must usually be of good size. A $100,000 boat is greater than 10 times more likely to become involved in maritime lien lawsuits than is one worth $10,000. Not only is it more valuable; its bills will usually be higher. Another influence is area of operation. Should a boat have been in a state not equipped with new laws, the maritime creditors might there be used to Admiralty law as their avenue of recovery. Removal of the boat to a new site need not discourage their persistence. Add the element of sizeable unpaid bills and a maritime lien action could result.

Assuming, then, that a buyer has a basis for concern, what precautions should he take? The status of maritime liens is hard to learn; for, as we've seen, they are secret and do not depend on possession. Knowing the area of previous operation would help; but when that should be a metropolitan sprawl of harbors and boat shops, what really is achieved? Telephone calls to 17 marine repair yards would not guarantee that the 18th did not have a claim. Best, perhaps, is to listen carefully after you ask the seller where and when he had work done on the boat. Then if there should develop uneasiness about unpaid bills, you have some clues. Remember that even should the law of a particular state require a special procedure for the recordation or enforcement of boat liens, such a law might not apply to out-of-state bills. Common sense says, "Be alert and be careful."

Of interest not only to the buyer, but to every boatowner, is some further comment on liens, maritime and otherwise. Generally speaking, the legal blackjack of a maritime lien stems from transactions which are considered maritime. And the building of a boat would seem to fit neatly in such a category. But it doesn't. A *building* contract is non-maritime under the American law of Admiralty. The boat, for contract purposes, is not a *she.* The shipyard does not get a maritime lien for its building efforts. Nor do its sub-contractors enjoy such a powerful aid. So if the boatyard doesn't pay all its bills, the buyer shouldn't anticipate a barrage from maritime lien claimants. A fair question now to ask is, "When does *it* become a *she?*

Trying to frame an answer points up both the frustrations and the fascinations of legal matters. Involved are words, intentions and reasoning. Neither computer program nor test tube will ever set such uniquely human factors into unequivocal array. There is an old seafaring story of the grouchy shipmaster who couldn't find his favorite teapot. He quizzed the steward to learn if it had been lost. Here was the steward's reply: "Since something is not lost if you know where it is, then the teapot is not lost. It is 10 miles astern in 600 fathoms of water." The word *lost* has shades of meaning. So does the word *completed* in reference to boat building. A general guide is that she is finished when she is ready as a structure for her intended use. So the builder of a tank which is to be fitted in a boat under construction is placing the tank in an *it.* He has no maritime lien. But the supplier of fuel to fill the tank delivers the liquid to a *her*. He can have a maritime lien.

After completion, though, she is clearly maritime. *Repair* work done by a boat yard does give rise to a maritime lien. Here, again, as with the lost teapot, shades of meaning can enter. If the repair is total rebuilding, she might revert to a legal pile of disconnected *its* for a while. But the normal pattern is that repair to a boat is a maritime activity.

We've already read that the steps to enforce maritime liens through Admiralty courts are complicated and expensive. So the practice in some areas is for creditors to rely on land law to recover. They either look to the general credit of the owner without taking dead aim on the boat; or they keep the vessel in their possession until the debt is paid.

New boating law on its trial trip in California seeks to lessen the worries over unpaid boat bills. A pattern is set both for possessory liens, (like the hotelman's claim on the guest's rucksack mentioned in the last chapter), and for those independent of possession. Section 490 of that state's Harbors and Navigation Code outlines the picture this way:

> "490. DEBTS CONTRACTED FOR BENEFIT OF VESSELS. DEBTS AMOUNTING TO AT LEAST FIFTY DOLLARS ($50), CONTRACTED FOR THE BENEFIT OF VESSELS, ARE LIENS IN THE CASES PROVIDED IN SECTION 491.
>
> ACTIONS FOR ANY OF THE CAUSES SPECIFIED IN SECTION 491 SHALL BE BROUGHT AGAINST THE OWNERS BY NAME, IF KNOWN, BUT IF NOT KNOWN, THAT FACT SHALL BE STATED IN THE COMPLAINT, AND THE DEFENDANTS SHALL BE DESIGNATED AS UNKNOWN OWNERS. OTHER PERSONS HAVING A LIEN UPON THE VESSEL MAY BE MADE DEFENDANTS IN THE ACTION, THE NATURE AND AMOUNT OF SUCH LIEN BEING STATED IN THE COMPLAINT."

Section *491* details the claims in these words:

> "491. LIABILITY AND LIENS FOR SERVICES, SUPPLIES, WORK, ETC. "ALL VESSELS ARE LIABLE FOR:
>
> A) SERVICES RENDERED ON BOARD AT THE REQUEST OF, OR UNDER CONTRACT WITH, THEIR RESPECTIVE OWNERS, MASTERS, AGENTS OR CONSIGNEES.
>
> B) SUPPLIES FURNISHED IN THIS STATE FOR THEIR USE, AT THE REQUEST OF THEIR RESPECTIVE OWNERS, MASTERS, AGENTS OR CONSIGNEES.

C) WORK DONE OR MATERIALS FURNISHED IN THIS STATE FOR THEIR CONSTRUCTION, REPAIR OR EQUIPMENT.
D) THEIR WHARFAGE AND ANCHORAGE WITHIN THIS STATE.
E) BREACH OF ANY CONTRACT FOR THE TRANSPORTATION OF PERSONS OR PROPERTY BETWEEN PLACES WITHIN THIS STATE, MADE BY THEIR RESPECTIVE OWNERS, MASTERS, AGENTS OR CONSIGNEES.
F) INJURIES CAUSED BY THEM TO PERSONS OR PROPERTY, IN THIS STATE, DEMANDS FOR THESE SEVERAL CAUSES CONSTITUTE LIENS UPON ALL VESSELS, HAVE PRIORITY IN THE ORDER ENUMERATED, AND HAVE PREFERENCE OVER ALL OTHER DEMANDS; BUT SUCH LIENS ONLY CONTINUE IN FORCE FOR THE PERIOD OF ONE YEAR FROM THE TIME THE CAUSE OF ACTION ACCRUED."

The sections which follow detail the lien provisions for particular creditors. For example, the master of a vessel is given a general lien, independent of possession, for necessary advances he has made or liability he has incurred for the vessel; however, he has no lien for wages. But his crewmembers are given a lien of highest priority for their wage claims. A lien is also given the Federal Government for damages to a buoy or beacon. And procedures to enforce these liens are spelled out. These provide for service of notice, seizure of the boat, owner intervention, sale of the vessel and distribution of proceeds to lien claimants.

Another section grants a *possessory lien* for such services as repairs, labor, supplies, storage and mooring. Included are detailed provisions for notice to the owner, sale of the boat to satisfy the lien and later redemption by the legal owner.

All of this sounds somewhat like claim-jumping; for these matters have historically been within the province of Admiralty. Yet there is really no violence done to that ancient Admiralty pattern. Flatly stated is that such rights and obligations created by state law are subordinate to any superseding federal law. But evident by the very existence of such statutes is the good purpose of fashioning legal procedures primarily for small vessels. These simplified state remedies tend to make the more cumbersome Federal recourse unattractive.

Actually the advent of such legislation brings clearing skies to the small craft world. . .and in a manner recalling the Baltic shipowners and merchants of centuries ago. Now, as then, involved persons had special problems which needed special regulation. And, as then, they worked together to establish a code to serve their particular situation. These modern boating "Laws of Wisbuy" point the way towards a truly separate branch of law for recreational and small boating.

Now, what about the boater who might not enjoy custom-made guidelines? For patterns such as in California are basically local routines. In his area, the picture might, for a while, remain more clouded by a mix of general Admiralty law and shoreside concepts in varying proportions. Some further mention of the high points of the Admiralty view is important to him. And that comment will also serve to guide everyone in those circumstances where the new statutes might not apply.

We've already encountered the *maritime lien* several times; and here it comes again. By general Admiralty, It is granted to quite a list of persons who do business with a ship. Repairmen, suppliers, crewmembers: they all get it for their unpaid bills and wages. And we will shortly learn that the list is quite a bit longer. These claims, remember, require neither recordation nor possession. Nor do they have a specific time limit. The claimant must not sleep on his rights; he is expected to be reasonably alert in presenting his lien. But what amounts to diligence or slumber varies with the facts of each case; and the Admiralty court does the deciding.

Not all such claims are of equal rank. Rather, they are assigned priorities by type and by time. High on the list are claims for wages, damages inflicted by the vessel and for salvage. Below them are charges for repairs and supplies. As to time, the procedure is somewhat surprising. Expected, perhaps, would be priority based on age of claim; he who is owed the longest should first be paid. But Admiralty law does it backwards. He who is the latest in time within a category tends to get paid first. And the theory makes some sense. A creditor who supplies paint in January makes it possible for the vessel to look more attractive to one who supplies fuel on credit in July. The complexities of *priorities* are not for us here to tangle with; for when the problem comes up, the court does the arranging. The concept, though, can at least become a conversation piece.

Now to the status of one who loans money on a boat. A normal pattern in financing is for the lender to take back a *mortgage* on property as security for his loan. Admiralty law, however, did not recognize that mortgage as a *maritime* lien. Such a lender ended up at the bottom of the pile, with all the maritime lien claimants perched on top of him. Obviously, this unfavorable situation put a damper on loans to vessels. So a special Federal law called the *Ship Mortgage Act* was passed to encourage maritime financing. By it, the lender who follows the procedural requirements of the statute receives a *preferred mortgage*,[2] he receives a maritime lien. This status, however, is only available when the vessel is *documented;* that is, when she is 5 net tons or more and has a document issued by the U.S. Coast Guard. More of that when we speak with the Customs Broker. But now we can define where such a lender appears in the priority ranking. His level cuts across the category of repairmen and suppliers. Those whose claims pre-date the recording of the preferred mortgage remain ahead of him. But those who thereafter do business with the vessel are presumed to have knowledge of the mortgage; so they come behind him. Banks and loan companies can use the preferred mortgage form when and only when a vessel is documented. The papers are then recorded at the *Marine Inspection Office of the U.S. Coast Guard;* and notice of the mortgage is attached to the ship's Coast Guard document. In other cases, the common practice is for the lender to require a *conditional sales contract* be executed. By it he can appear as legal owner of the boat and more effectively control her legal status during the period of the loan.

Now to summarize what our conversation so far has developed. Vessels of 5 net tons or more can have available the documentation procedure of the U.S. Coast Guard. Title and mortgage records are filed with the Marine Inspection Office of the Coast Guard District at the vessel's

[2] *See page 87*

home port. And specified forms and procedures are required to complete the paper work. Such a vessel can be held subject to a preferred mortgage, by which the lender receives a maritime lien. And to a great extent, that boat is in the general stream of Admiralty law. Boats which are either not eligible to be documented or do not elect to do so, are in a category subject to state or Federal numbering statutes. How extensive those patterns are can vary from state to state. They can be as sparse as just identification procedures tied in with local tax collection; they can be as comprehensive as establishment of a special legal structure for many phases of the business side of boats.

When the coverage is as wide as under new boating law, there is almost a total alternative to general Admiralty procedures. . .at least for business within one state. When the local law is meager, there can exist a sort of local option condition mixing general Admiralty law with land-type procedures in amounts greatly influenced by local practice.

In print the picture appears much more mottled than in actual use; for all segments of the boating field want simple, predictable patterns. Variations are more evident when the procedures of one area are contrasted with those of another. But the approach of the boater, wherever he is located, remains somewhat the same. He starts with his general understanding of how business is conducted ashore. To that he adds the details of what his state or area might have created specifically for small boats. And then he places it all in the setting of a discussion such as ours on the general theme of Admiralty law. The result will be a basis for judging when he is heading for stormy seas, and when he should engage professional aid as pilot.

Next on deck is a topic of great importance. Not true anymore is the tired statement that if you must ask how much a yacht costs you can't afford to own one. The joys of pleasure boating are no longer just limited to the very rich. Keeping tabs on expense is now stylish. And means to soften the financial burden are very attractive. Sooner or later, in casting about for ways to make the going easier, an owner will probably consider this thought: why not rent his boat every once in a while to responsible people? Giving up its use for a few weekends each year shouldn't intrude too much on recreation; and the extra dollars will certainly lessen financial strain. He should, though, watch his helm, for dangerous legal waters lie ahead. We'd better take a close look for the shoals and reefs.

To begin with, there are no general prohibitions against hiring your boat out for a legal purpose. No reminder is necessary that everything is wrong with a deal involving an illegal activity. But to turn the boat over to a person who seems reputable for what appears to be a fair and legal purpose is legitimate business. Where the rub comes is in the circumstances.

What we are now to talk about is *chartering.* The shoreside parallel to this type of contract is a lease; and its proper maritime name is *charter party.* Ownership carries with it some pretty obvious rights. The boatowner can, within reasonable limits, operate his boat when, where, how and why he wishes. By a charter party he turns over to another some or all of those rights.

By a *bareboat* charter the owner in effect surrenders all control. He lets the charterer act as owner during the period of the contract. Fuel, stores, supplies, repairs, crew . . . they are supplied by the charterer. At the end of the period he returns the boat to the owner in the same condition as received, reasonable wear and tear excepted.

There are two other kinds of charters which we'll label and define; but neither will get much further attention here. By a *time charter* the use of the vessel is reserved to the charterer for a period of time; but the owner actually retains control. Under a *voyage charter*, the term of the agreement is measured, not in time units, but by a specified passage from one place to another. As with the time charter, the owner retains control.

It is the *bareboat charter* which is particularly in point for us. And it appears to be as simple as this: *A* lets *B* use the boat as his own for the period of the contract. Simple things, though, have a habit of becoming complex in a hurry. In this case, for example, the owner must be sure the charter will not mix up his insurance coverage. We'll talk more of this when we reach the chapter on insurance. But thoughts, meanwhile, can be put in mind. Does the insurance contract cover a charterer's use? How can the owner assure that the charterer stays within any cruising limits of the policy? What if he doesn't and runs into trouble?

Insurance is just one of the facets of the problem. Another consideration is the *warranty of seaworthiness.* Unless the charter specifies otherwise, the owner can be viewed as representing the boat as ready in all respects for the charterer's intended use. Should there be a defect, (even if unknown to the owner), storm flags can fly. More restful is the owner who has clearly stated in the agreement that the condition of the boat is not warranted and that the charterer accepts her after his own inspection. Nor should the charterer be too casual about the deal. On the other side of every right is a balancing weight of responsibility. He is going to be a boatowner for a while. And he has duties not only to the real owner, but also to the rest of the seafaring world. The status of *his* insurance coverage certainly bears checking.

A charter party is an important contract involving a valuable property capable of doing extensive damage. Both sides of the arrangement should view it as far more serious than a friendly accommodation.

Mention of friendly accommodation brings us to the case of the *boat borrower.* Anyone who asks to use your boat is either unaware of what he asks, or is dangerously unconcerned. You as owner will have responsibility to everyone, including the borrower. Yet you have trusted the performance of those duties to another. What the situation comes down to is almost a blank check drawn on your assets. Don't lend your boat to anyone, whether kith, kin or otherwise. No informed person will think less of you for it.

Back, though, to the *bareboat charter* as a means to pick up some expense money. Let's conjure up a set of facts to see how the situation could develop. *A,* a boatowner, frequently invites *B* to cruise with him on weekends. During their trips, *B* assists in operation and shows a competent skill in handling the boat. Then one day *B* approaches *A* with this proposition. *B* and some fellow employees plan a fishing trip. They would like to charter *A's* boat for two days. The agreement would be in writing, and only after adequate insurance protection and other safeguards had been arranged. *A* would not go on the trip, nor would he have any measure of control over the outing. *B* would be in full charge. He would see to the fueling and supplies; he would operate the boat.

This setup would seem to propose a straightforward bareboat charter. On one side, an owner bargains away rights of ownership during the time of the contract; on the other, a group assumes temporary responsibility of ownership. So the charter is arranged, and the trip works out to the satisfaction of everyone. In fact, the deal is so satisfactory that *B* and his friends offer to repeat the pattern once a month throughout the year. *A* might seem to be in the part-time business of chartering his boat; but nothing is necessarily wrong with that.

Now, though, let's change the facts a little. *B* and his friends still would like to use the boat; but *A* is not at all satisfied with the competence of any of them to take over operation. He would like to receive the charter money, but he wouldn't feel that the boat would be in safe hands. Of course, if he were to go along and run the boat, there would be no problem. *B's* group is agreeable, so why not? Why not, indeed! If *A* does so he will destroy the bareboat charter. And in the process he will probably end up *carrying passengers for hire.* With that status, he meets the full force of Coast Guard regulations for small passenger vessels. A Coast Guard *Certificate of Inspection* for the boat could be necessary; and an *Operator's license* for A could be required. Neither of these documents is just issued cavalierly after a casual inquiry. The boat's certificate requires compliance with regulations governing such factors as construction, stability, safety equipment, machinery, electrical equipment...and in a fashion far more stringent than a courtesy examination. To acquire the Operator's license requires documentation of a specified minimum experience, of physical capability and of professional competence. Involved can be a comprehensive examination taking from 3 hours to several days for completion. When the American public is transported, the American standards for personnel and equipment are among the highest in the world. We all take this for granted when we board an air liner. The pattern is no different when buying passage on a boat. Were *A,* the boatowner, to go with *B's* group on an outing, he would probably be considered by the Coast Guard as a professional offering transportation for hire. And without the proper license and certification, he would be subject to severe penalties.

So the parties try to figure out a way around the regulations. All involved, they think, is a fun outing with everyone compatible and aware of the situation. No one should be inclined to make a "Federal case" out of an occasional friendly boat trip. In deference, though, to red tape, they consider a few possibilities. They could, perhaps, charter the boat and then hire *A* for the trip. He could be paid for his trouble; and he would be the legal employee of the temporary owners under the charter. No good! *A* really has not surrendered control sufficiently to preserve the bareboat charter.

If that won't work, then why don't they hire some third-party skipper of competent repute? This is not so bad; but *A* might still be asking for trouble. For, since in most cases he would be suggesting that person and would have the last word on selection . . . there might still not be sufficient surrender of control. The usual pattern of these arrangements is that the group really only wants a boat trip. Each member is actually just buying transportation on *A's* boat operated in a manner satisfactory to *A*.

The Coast Guard takes a very sophisticated attitude towards such an arrangement. And a boat owner who attempts camouflage of its true character is foolish. Sooner or later he is going to be in trouble. For he really is, too often, in the business of carrying for hire. No amount of deception will alter the legal situation. Individuals pay a pro-rate of a set price to take a ride on a boat. Perhaps one group member will buy the beer and another will pick up the pretzels; but the boatowner is at the bottom of *vessel control*.

Now we've hit upon the key. . . this matter of control. And in nearly all of these gentle frauds, the boatowner does, in fact, retain it. One might criticize our analysis as too harsh. Yet it is far better to err on the cautious side. Actual intention must be crystal clear. Does the owner really agree to deliver his boat to the *exclusive* control of the group with nary a strand of rope attached? If so, we should apologize for our suspicions and say, "Que via con Dios."

But most of the time the facts are otherwise. *A* wants the group to have a safe and enjoyable outing, and he wants the boat to come back undamaged. So he sort of oversees the voyage. Rationalizing, he believes that he serves everyone's best interests. Yet all his high-minded concern for recreation in efficiency and safety can be reduced to one phrase: carrying passengers for hire. Not he, but the Coast Guard, establishes and enforces standards of care in that field.

This side of boat ownership deserves the closest attention. Advice of experienced counsel has obvious value. And discussing the matter with the District Coast Guard Office is not giving away the game plan. Outline what you have in mind and the applicable rules will be spelled out for you. This is not a game of hide-and-seek. Try to make it one and you will surely lose. Ulysses was tied to the mast to defeat the sweet song of the Sirens. To be bound hand and foot on the foredeck might not be required of the boatowner; but certainly he should be extremely wary of this situation.

So far, in our glances at purchase, sale, agreements to build or repair and at charters, we have been discussing factors in the legal field of contracts. Now we will enter another department, that of the *tort*. This strange term originates, perhaps, in the same place as *tortuous* and *torsion* . . . a twisting out of normal or rightful paths. And in law it describes an injury which is inflicted without right. It is not the same as a crime where emphasis is on offenses against society by breaking a rule of conduct required of the society's members.

Here we encounter a *civil wrong* and the legal rules to place the burden of loss on the one responsible for the act. What it all amounts to is the boatowner's liability for *accidental injury or damage*. And our discussion will be in two segments. First to consider are injuries or damage suffered by people and things on board the boat. Then we'll handle such losses suffered by the rest of the world.

Aside from the owner and his family, the persons who will be aboard a pleasure boat can be grouped this way: *guests, licensees, crewmembers* and *trespassers.* We didn't mention paying passengers; for by now the idea is clear that they shouldn't be aboard at all. But the responsibility owed to a passenger can serve as the starting point for our discussion. A *passenger-for-hire* is to receive the highest degree of care. The owner doesn't insure his safety; but he certainly is required to use great foresight in protecting his charge from injury. At the other end of the spectrum is a trespasser. He is uninvited, unpaid and unwanted. Towards him the owner has no responsibility other than not willfully to harm him. The groups in the middle, though, are not so simply handled. Let's first see how the owner stands relative to a *guest*.

Not surprising is that there are two opposite schools of thought. The owner might like to analyze things this way. Motivated by good fellowship, he graciously offers the gangway to his friend. The guest is not obliged to accept; but when he does, he should expect nothing more than what the owner provides for himself. It would seem highly unfair to hold the owner responsible for injury or damage suffered by a free-loading companion. Of course, the guest, standing at the other end of the gangway, would rather not agree. He might consider it a strange world if he cannot expect the owner to exercise reasonable care towards those whom, unsolicited, he invites to ride on his boat. Usually, though, there is little difference of opinion on one point. Friendship falls overboard when a lawsuit appears on deck.

But still to consider is which view of the *owner-guest* relationship might prevail. Many courts side more or less with the guest. The owner has been held to owe the guest *reasonable care.* Should an injury be suffered because of some careless or negligent act of the owner, then that tort could bring liability. Again, though, like the "lost" teapot, the definition of *reasonable* has a variety of hues. When the conduct is wilful, there is no dispute. And usually the question of reckless or grossly negligent action is easily answered. But reasonable is another matter. When an owner has been held liable, there has usually been conduct not up to the standards of normal good sense. An explosion caused by improper venting of fuel vapors is an example. Another is a fall due to a skid on an oily deck. The general approach is to set standards in relation to conditions. Fuel vapors really should be vented and decks really should not be oily. That a *guest* was blown overboard or took the fall is not so much the point. These conditions should not be allowed to exist for anyone rightfully aboard.

New boating law as being tried in California (Section *661.1* of that state's Harbors and Navigation Code) seems to support the owner by these words:

> "661.1 LIABILITY TO GUEST ON VESSEL. NO PERSON WHO AS A GUEST ACCEPTS A RIDE IN ANY VESSEL UPON THE WATERS OF THE STATE WITHOUT GIVING COMPENSATION FOR SUCH A RIDE, OR ANY OTHER PERSON HAS ANY RIGHT OF ACTION FOR

CIVIL DAMAGES AGAINST THE OPERATOR OF THE VESSEL OR AGAINST ANY OTHER PERSON LEGALLY LIABLE FOR THE CONDUCT OF THE OPERATOR ON ACCOUNT OF PERSONAL INJURY TO OR THE DEATH OF THE GUEST DURING THE RIDE, UNLESS THE PLAINTIFF IN SUCH ACTION ESTABLISHES THAT THE INJURY OR DEATH PROXIMATELY RESULTED FROM THE INTOXICATION OR WILLFUL MISCONDUCT OF THE OPERATOR OR ESTABLISHES THAT SUCH OPERATOR WAS UNDER THE INFLUENCE OF ANY NARCOTIC DRUG, BARBITUATE OR MARIJUANA. AS USED IN THIS SECTION A "GUEST" SHALL BE DEEMED TO INCLUDE ANY PERSON OR PERSONS BEING TOWED BY ANY VESSEL ON WATER SKIS OR AN AQUAPLANE OR A SIMILAR DEVICE."

No owner, though, should rest on his oars because of such a statute. Note that the section just quoted limits its effect to ". . . the waters of the state." The meaning of that phrase is not clear enough for comfort. It would seem to cover California's totally intra-state Lake Arrowhead; and San Francisco Bay should not present a problem. What, though, is to be said about the cruising area of Mexico's Baja California? Can it be considered subject to the laws of our California?

Before we form any opinion on owner's liability in this field, we must consider another type of person aboard . . . the *business visitor*. Sometimes the term *business guest* is used to describe him; on occasion he has borne the label of licensee. There are technical differences at times; but the class in general is not hard to pin down. These are the people who come aboard to transact business with the owner. They might be present to deliver supplies; or, perhaps, they are attracted by a "For Sale" sign. The California statute might have them in mind when, in the third line, it says ". . . or any other person". And if that is so, then the new law places them in the guest category. Generally speaking, that is where they fit in most areas; although some courts say they deserve no other warning than that of hidden dangers. The simpler view is that anyone other than a paying passenger and a trespasser should be grouped with guests.

Now for that opinion. *Reasonable care* should not be considered a commodity to be rationed in measured amounts depending on the person and the locale. A half-teaspoon for one group, a full teaspoon for another and a double portion for still a third is foolishness. The owner will seldom go astray if he uses himself and family as the guidelines. He would not like to be sitting on gas fumes or walking on a slippery deck. In fact, he would not like to be near any avoidable hazards. Part of the package of ownership is proper maintenance and safe operation. When such is attended to, the owner will have few liability worries. This might sound like repetition of the obvious: be careful and you will be exercising reasonable care. Yet there is really no other answer to avoidance of the whole problem. None of us, though, are so free of error that we can disregard human lapses. The most prudent of owners will at some time or other overlook an item of importance. So insurance protection becomes essential.

A routine followed by some very careful owners is to request guests to sign a simply-worded *release of liability.* The thinking is that today's guest is well aware of what can develop in our complex society, so he will not be outraged when he is asked to place his host at ease. There is scant basis for criticism of such an approach. In order to make the pattern appear as Standard Operating Procedure, one might say that the "Insurance Company" requires it. And for little cost, an attorney can draft an understandable, short form. Realistically, of course, many owners might consider such a pattern as too unfriendly and business-like for pleasure boating. Perhaps if the insurance company really did require that such be done, everyone would be more at ease. At least, though, the procedure should be considered and its propriety carefully weighed.

We have another group of persons aboard to consider: the *crew*. To many of us, the problem might seem illusory; for all it takes is a different cap insignia to transform the owner from Captain to Cabin Steward. But the term *crew* does not just apply to a score of liveried and paid employees on a stately pleasure barge. There are quite a few arrangements by which an unpaid helper could be classed as a seaman entitled to legal rights granted to crewmembers. Here is an example to justify a second glance at this phase of boating law. Suppose an owner plans a passage from Port A to Port B, a dozen miles away. He meets a person who professes some small boat experience and wishes to go along. No pay is involved and all to be expected of the companion is to give a hand enroute. During the trip, the *"work-away"* is injured. And the boat owner might well be a very reluctant employer in the eyes of Admiralty law. Even if the likelihood of such a trip is small, we should investigate the relationship between the owner and crewmember.

We're not about to wrap this phase of our discussion in a skinny paragraph with a glossary of technical terms bobbing along astern. Instead, we must head off again into a sketch of historical background.

Those who serve a ship have always been viewed as working under quite unusual conditions. The physical limits of the vessel so confine their movements that, to begin with, they seem to have accepted a degree of voluntary imprisonment. Moreover, the needs of the vessel must be of first concern. Choosing to take the day off, or declining extra work at midnight is just not possible. The description of "being married to the job" is apt.

Long ago, that marriage was, to a great extent, for better or for worse. The seaman was expected to do his best in the service of the ship and in return he received board, room and a not-too-princely wage. When he suffered injury aboard, his remedies against the owner or the ship were few. What rights he had, though, have survived to the present time. . . with significant additions.

For centuries the seaman has enjoyed the owner's *warranty of seaworthiness.* We've already met this term; and now a closer look is necessary. By it the owner represents the vessel as being suitable for her intended use. In effect, he states that she is capable of safe navigation. This warranty is not limited to the owner-crew relationship. It can apply, as we've seen, to charters and to several other situations. But for crewmen it was almost the sole protection available against dangerous working conditions. If a seaman fell from aloft because the ship rolled excessively while he was so exposed, his damage suit against the owner might well have been fruitless. But if he could show that, anticipating such rolling, the owner should have fitted grab rails or other protective devices, then the result might have changed. For he would then contend the vessel had not been seaworthy as warranted. He would not complain that his injury resulted from the owner's carelessness, so his lawsuit would not be for a tort. Nor would he really be saying that the owner broke the employment contract by not giving him a safe place to work. Instead, he would say there had been no agreement to work in the first place, for the owner had misrepresented a basic fact.

Today an injured crewman can still sue the vessel in Admiralty for breach of that warranty. And for the past half century he has enjoyed additional remedies under a law called the *Jones Act.* By it he can effectively sue the owner personally for negligence, with the action not limited to a libel filed in an Admiralty court.

Stemming from ancient times are three further rights very much alive today. They are called *wages, maintenance* and *cure;* and they began as forerunners of today's workmen's compensation laws. An example will show what is involved. A seaman is injured while in the service of his ship; and the cause was his carelessness without any fault of the ship or her owner. But the fact is he is out of commission for a while. By these age-old rules, the owner is expected to help tide him over during the period of recovery. Entitlement is to *maintenance,* or funds for board and room while ailing, and to *cure,* which is payment of medical expenses. In addition he can receive full *wages* until he is again ready to work, or until the term of employment would normally end. . . whichever occurs first. And to enforce these rights the seaman can sue the ship or the shipowner.

So the present-day crewmember has a well-stocked arsenal of legal weapons with no fixed limit on recovery. He can sue ship or owner in Admiralty; he can sue the owner personally in other courts as well. He can sue for breach of the warranty of seaworthiness; he can sue for negligence; he can, regardless of who might be at fault, sue for wages, maintenance and cure. And neither state nor Federal workmen's compensation laws will apply.

The boatowner should weigh carefully *any* proposal for work to be done on his boat. A boatyard worker is no hazard; for his employer is really the boatyard, and not the owner. But a casual worker who, for $2 an hour, will do odd jobs of painting might well be a threat. It could be expensive, indeed, to pay room, board and medical expense for such a disabled "seaman" while his broken leg is knitting.

Here is an area where the new boating laws seem not to establish a clear alternative to the general Admiralty procedures. Section *491* of California's Harbors and Navigation Code, (quoted on page 18), makes "...all vessels" liable for "...(f) injuries caused by them to the persons or property, in this state." But it doesn't by any means seem to set up a detailed procedure. Perhaps the problem is not considered significant enough in the small craft world. It is far better for all hands to accept that Admiralty and all its trimmings show through this gap. Again, insurance is an answer.

Now to the second part of our discussion of owner liability. What about injuries or damage inflicted to persons or things not on board? The majority of problems here arise from *collision*. . .damaging contact between your boat and the rest of the planet. And the total cure is not to have one. Sometimes quoted nowadays is a statement attributed to an ancient Greek: "A collision at sea can spoil your entire day." And to avoid such trauma, various sets of regulations described generally as *Rules of the Road* have been prepared. Discussion of the ins and outs of those requirements is not feasible here. Comprehensive treatment will be found in many boating manuals...for example, **MARINER'S NOTEBOOK**. Comment here is directed to the subject of liability when a collision has taken place.

General Admiralty law requires that the court answer two questions in a collision case: who is liable and how should the losses be borne. On a highway, unforeseeable causes can sometimes produce inevitable accidents. An example would be a faulty traffic light. But the likelihood afloat is much higher. And the most common circumstance is weather: wind, current and storm. So the boat is not always going to be held liable for collision damage it might inflict. An *Act of God* can intervene to upset the most reasonably careful navigation. Since God is not responsive to lawsuits, the courts will then leave the parties as they are, each to lick his own wounds.

But *inevitable accident* is not used as a convenient excuse or casual explanation. The injuring boat must satisfy the court that things happened in spite of any reasonable care which the situation would require. In turn, the measure of that care is fashioned in the context of the accident. A small craft pummelled and tossed by squally seas will not be judged by standards required of a larger, more stable vessel. A radar-equipped boat will be considered more informed than one relying only on sound signals in fog. The net result is that although God might get into the Act more often afloat than ashore, such a concept of divine intervention is no scapegoat.

A key rule of American Admiralty is this: when a vessel, at the time of a collision, is in actual violation of a rule of the road, it is presumed that such a fault contributed to the accident. And that vessel will then bear the heavy burden of proving, not just that the violation might not have caused the accident, nor probably did not cause the accident. . .but that it could not have done so. It is, then, important that all requirements of *Rules of the Road* be fulfilled. Here is a for instance. A boat at anchor in fog is run down by a vessel proceeding at very high speed. Fault clearly lies with the speeder. But the boat at anchor wasn't sounding a bell signal required by Rules of the Road. How might that anchored boat fare? Probably not too well.

She would like to contend that no muffled clang of a bell would have made any difference because of the other boat's speed. And the judge might be sympathetic. Despite such anguish, though, he would still probably hold the anchored boat partly at fault. She would have to show that the bell could not have made a difference. And that burden would be too heavy to carry. For the bell could have made a difference. *Could* comes from *can;* and *can* suggests *capable of.* The key is not probability as much as possibility. *Strict* compliance with the Rules of the Road is the answer. This is not just limited to sections involving "privilege" and "burden;" it includes running lights, bells, foghorns and all the specified equipment.

Having learned the anchored boat could be partly to blame, we next must consider how the amount of damage might be handled. First of all, when damage is partial, the Admiralty court will use the cost of repair as its guide. When, though, a vessel is totally lost, the measure is her *market value* just prior to the loss. Owners can have mixed emotions in such cases. If a vessel cost $5,000 five years before but had a fair market value of $10,000 the day before her loss, the owner might be pleased with the outcome. But the facts could be reversed. Perhaps after purchase for $5,000 the owner had spent another $5,000 to make her suit his own individual tastes. Yet, because his idea of improvements differed from those of most buyers, her value prior to the loss was only $3,000. He could consider himself unjustly treated. The general rule, though, for a total loss is market value. It would appear that if one has to lose his boat by collision, he should do so when the market is Bullish and not in the days of the Bears.

Back to the problem of partial loss. Suppose in our example that the anchored boat suffered $1,000 damage and the speeder's repair would be $3,000. Further, suppose the judge has decided that although the speeder was the major cause, the boat at anchor must also bear some burden. What next? What comes next is a refreshing instance of legal evolution.

The Common Law of England required that he who sought damages from his fellows be, himself, innocent of fault. Any stain of his negligence would say he contributed to his own loss. The concept of contributory negligence would bar him from any recovery, without inquiry into the relative value of his contributing fault. This pattern, transplanted to our land, became the majority rule in our shoreside courts. It has been subject to erosion, and the trend to change is growing. But if the anchored boat were to seek justice in a court applying that rule, he would receive nothing.

Admiralty, though, has regularly pursued another direction. It will apportion damages between vessels held both at fault. The seagoing view, one of comparative negligence, is considered the better. But until recently, the way American Admiralty applied the doctrine produced some bizarre results. For well over a century the American view was that mutual fault brought equal burden. When two parties were negligent, we would total the damages and then divide by two. Each would bear half the loss. During that era, our Quiet Man at anchor would have been foolish to have sought Admiralty relief. His $1,000 damage, added to the speeder's $3,000, would total $4,000. American Admiralty could have charged each with a $2,000 burden. In effect, the anchored boat would have paid $1,000 to the speeder to equalize the loss. In turn, the errant speeder would have broken all records to reach the sanctuary of American Admiralty and its unique windfall.

Other maritime nations have for most of this century gone on a different tack. They have made an effort, when possible, to establish the degrees of fault and then assessed damages accordingly. In mid-1975 the

U.S. Supreme Court changed our inequitable pattern to follow suit.

So by our new rule judgment in Admiralty is based, when possible, on the degree of fault attributed to each party. What deduction would be made for our soft-spoken friend's silence at anchor is hard to predict. Perhaps it might be worth $250. Surely, though, it would no longer allow the speeder to sail off with an undeserved advantage.

All law is nicked by such blemishes, and some are still uncorrected. The subject, of course, is one for attorneys to fret over. But an owner should at least appreciate the general problem. Then he can better accept why his attorney might use one court when, in a case "just like it" last year, suit was filed in another.

Any vessel has the capability of wreaking enormous damage and exposing her owner to large legal claims. So early in the game, Admiralty began to develop a means to relieve the strain. In the United States, this relief is afforded by a law called the *Limitation of Liability Act.* And its general effect is to allow an owner, under specified conditions, to limit his liability to the value of his vessel. Even though its original preamble stated that the intent was to encourage shipping, the statute has been held applicable to pleasure vessels. The mechanics of how it works are quite complicated. . . so much so that it would serve no purpose for us to wade too deeply into the subject. But the special conditions necessary to its application need mention.

Most relevant to pleasure boatowners is this exclusion: if the owner has, to some extent, personally participated in the fault causing the loss, he cannot limit liability. And for most pleasure boat situations the advantage has just evaporated. It is only fair to say that in the majority of cases developing in the recreational world, limitation of liability is not available. And the reason is obvious. Most of the time the owner will be closely involved with the negligent act which caused the loss. In fact, he probably will be at the helm himself. Yet it is not by any means an empty right; for not always will that owner be so present and aware of the carelessness. Our aim is to identify and summarize concepts. Here, then, is another. Avoiding its working parts, we'll leave further dissection to lawyers and insurance underwriters.

Now, what does the new boating law do in this area? It remains silent on the subject of suits against the boatowner for injury or damage inflicted when the owner personally participates in the casualty. Apparently the idea is to leave the parties to shoreside or Admiralty law as spirit and circumstances might move.

California's section *661,* however, outlines a limitation of liability pattern for cases when the owner is not the operator. In substance, here is the gist. An owner of an undocumented vessel numbered under the California code is liable for death or injury to persons and damage to property when his boat is negligently operated by any person using the boat with the permission, expressed or implied, of the owner. When the operator is a member of the owner's immediate family, permission is presumed. And the negligence of the actual operator in any of these cases is imputed to the owner.

Then, though, the limitations come: a maximum of $10,000 for death of or injury to one person in one accident; a maximum of $20,000 total for deaths or injuries in that one accident; a maximum of $10,000 total for property damage caused in that one accident. The owner who is held liable under this section has the right to sue the actual operator for reimbursement. And specifically stated is protection for a seller who might appear of record as legal owner. A finance company is not to be involved in this liability just because it remains as owner of record for security reasons.

The answer, as usual, is insurance. And it should be noted that just insurance enough to cover limits as set out in a state code section might not be adequate. The one mentioned above limits liability only when the owner is *not* the actual operator. In other, and more common, cases, the ceiling is not set.

Damage claims do not have to arise just from collisions between vessels. A boat can hit a dock, an aid to navigation, a bridge or an assortment of other non-vessel structures. Nor need there be any physical contact. Propeller wash, for example, can be the cause of the liability. Colliding with an aid to navigation requires not only that the boatowner promptly notify the Coast Guard; he must also prepare to pay in full for the damages. And in such cases, proceedings can be taken directly against the vessel.

The general view, though, is that when a *non-maritime structure* is damaged, its owner cannot sue in an Admiralty court. Often what next transpires is that the boatowner finds a basis to have the suit transferred to Admiralty. . . with its havens of comparative negligence, divided damages and limitation of liability. Here again is a sector best left to the ingenuity of attorneys.

Now for a review of *shipwreck* and *salvage*. First let's consider the problem of a boat that is, for practical purposes, destroyed. She might have sunk or have been mortally impaled on a rocky shore. But either way she is finished as a boat. Now what? Well, by her insurance policy she might be viewed as "sold to the underwriters." When the insurance company is required to pay a total loss, it receives from the owner his rights in the hulk. What, though, about the rest of the world? What other interests are involved?

Should the wreck be on the bottom of the High Seas, then the story could well be finished. Davey Jones, custodian of the Deep, is quite permissive. He just shrugs casually as a wreck glides by on its way down. But when a boat has sunk in *navigable waters* under the control of a government, the procedures are different. Often the owner finds the wreck as difficult to shed as flypaper. For there is a definite national interest in maintaining waterways clear for navigation. In our country, the *Corps of Engineers of the U.S. Army* administers laws passed to preserve and protect our navigable waters. It has the power to remove *sunken vessels* obstructing or endangering navigation. After a specified time, the Army Engineers can clear the area by whatever means necessary to get rid of the wreck. Any salvaged pieces are then disposed of by the Army. Of course, if the wreck seriously interferes with navigation, then removal can start immediately. In such a case, the owner himself can be directed to do the job; and if he doesn't, the Army can charge the expense of removal against any salvaged value of the boat.

So, when his boat sinks in our navigable waters, the owner can't act like Davey Jones. If the remains constitute an immediate impediment to navigation, he might receive a notice to remove. Otherwise, he can use a procedure for *legal abandonment.* Of course, he should remember that he might now be dealing with a property which belongs to his insurance company. Keeping it advised of notices received, and requesting instructions for further action is a must to assure no problems in settlement of the loss. Should the boat have sunk in waters of a foreign country, the owner must seek advice from a U.S. Consul. Whatever procedures might be required by that nation must be followed in order to avoid further problems.

While all this sparring is going on, though, the owner has another duty. He must mark the location as a wreck. If he does not do so in U.S. waters, then the Coast Guard might do the job for him. . .and send a bill of so much a day for the buoy.

Consideration must also be given to local title record and taxation regulations. California, for example, requires that the owner of an undocumented boat give notice to the proper state agency when his boat is wrecked, destroyed or abandoned. And when she is documented by the U.S. Coast Guard, notification must be given to the home port Marine Inspection Office so that records there can be amended.

All this, like other procedures we discuss, is often reduced to a settled routine that starts in motion automatically when a wreck is reported. Even so, every owner knowing the outlines of his duties can avoid expensive missteps.

Not all casualties need end in disaster, of course. Nearly every owner will exert great effort to avoid the loss of his boat. In fact, his insurance policy expects that he minimize damage as much as is reasonably possible.. What aid, though, can he anticipate from others? The answer to that question brings us to the topic of *salvage.*

Mariners have the highest moral and legal obligations to assist in an attempt to save life without expectation of reward. The theory is that all of us share the hazards of the sea and must join forces to protect each other from its dangers. But togetherness stops there; let the elements take hull and deckhouse so long as lives are saved. Scant moral or legal obligation to save property is forced upon us. Some premium is necessary to justify extraordinary effort to save the ship; and that bonus is a salvage award.

There seems to be a tendency to classify salvors as predatory villains, skulking among whitecaps to pounce on the defenseless. There are, surely, instances of opportunistic gain from the misfortune of others. Yet, in context, such is really a superficial view. The concept of salvage arises, as does much of Admiralty law, from the field of commerce. A shipmaster in command of a vessel carrying merchandise for hundreds of shippers cannot blithely risk or even delay all those interests in order to preserve endangered property to which he owes no duty. The salvor, in that light, appears far different from a bird of prey. Instead, he emerges as one faced squarely by the dilemma of duty versus a normal inclination to help. The salvage award was fashioned to meet his problem. The mariner who voluntarily acts to save a vessel in danger and succeeds in his efforts is given a claim for his trouble. And all those involved in the task share the benefit. So the shipmaster who leaves his normal course of business to undertake the job can justify that action to his owner, shippers and to whomever else might, without consultation, have been at risk in the process.

There are three general prerequisites for the claim. First of all, the vessel assisted must have been in distress. There must be some reason to perform the service. And the one who decides that issue is the person in charge of the troubled boat. If he doesn't think he needs a salvor, then he cannot be forced to accept one. But once having taken the aid, he cannot lightly change his mind. Admiralty law is well aware of the Monday Morning Quarterback whose hindsight knows what play should have been called on the day before. And Admiralty law is no more inclined than a football referee to allow the game to be replayed. The decision of the person in command is viewed in the light of his then circumstances. And unless there is the strongest justification, the court will pay scant heed to any reconsideration.

The second requirement is that the salvor be a volunteer. One cannot expect bonus pay for doing a service he is already obliged to perform. So neither captain nor crewmember can be salvor of his own ship. Since neither a passenger nor a guest has an express duty to the ship, it could be said that either might be entitled to a salvage claim. But the law is not nearly so definite. Sometimes it says, "Yes" and then, again, sometimes the answer is "No." Since they are on board and in a position to aid, passengers and guests are often expected to turn to without need of any coaxing. But they might be rewarded for deeds above and beyond what is reasonably expected.

If someone contracts in advance of his aid to receive payment, then the voluntary element is absent; for he assumes an obligation to assist. Sometimes such an arrangement is called *contract salvage.* And payment can range from so much per day, win or lose, to the equivalent of full salvage payable only if successful.

The third condition for true salvage is success. The service performed must have benefited the endangered boat. This requirement is often described as "no cure, no pay." But the cure need not be complete. The salvor might still be awarded a premium if he has significantly improved the situation.

How much the salvor receives is up to the court. And the complex formula applied can be reduced to these questions: what was saved? what was risked? what dangers were encountered? what labor was performed? Whatever his award, though, the salvor receives with it a maritime lien of high priority. . .senior, for example, to both suppliers and mortgagees. This is only fair, since the service rendered preserves the security of both groups.

Again, insurance can be the owner's protection. But the owner should be familiar with what the policy requires of him. No underwriter is eager to pay off a salvage award that could have been avoided or at least minimized by an alert boatowner.

The complications of salvage are many, and to capture all of them here is neither feasible nor worthwhile. Enough for us to recognize what salvage is and how it comes into play.

When speaking of wrecks, we mentioned the term *abandonment*. It returns again for further study. What if you should come upon a vessel floating crewless on the High Seas? What if this should take place within U.S. waters? What if the boat is not afloat, but stranded, with no sign of life around? "What if's . . ." could go on and on. But all of them will usually add up to less than "Finders, Keepers." Neither High Seas nor national waters are such wildernesses that rights of ownership can so easily be forfeited. In each case the finder would probably be viewed somewhat as a salvor. And his labors in securing the vessel would give rise to a sort of salvage claim. Should no one come forward to claim ownership, then the finder might well end up as owner. But the pattern would be more of a purchase by his labor, rather than a staking of claim on abandoned property. And when the locale is within the geographical limits of some government, then local requirements can apply. Property that is "found" usually falls under procedures for impound, notice, sale and disposition. It is naive in our world to believe that things of value will often be viewed like unbranded Frontier cattle.

The afternoon is drawing to a close, and we have only one more subject to discuss with counsel. What about *crimes?* When something antisocial occurs aboard, whose police is summoned and whose law is broken? The key is the answer to a third question: where did the offense take place?

Our Federal District Courts have jurisdiction over crimes committed on the High Seas aboard vessels owned by U.S. citizens. If the boat is then within the waters of a state, the affair is a matter for the authorities of that state to handle. If the location is in foreign waters, then the proceeding can be under the laws of a foreign country.

Our purpose is served by recognition of the problems involved and then emphasis on the steps which prudence might demand. If something of this nature occurs while outside the jurisdiction of a state or of a foreign country, then, upon arrival at a U.S. harbor, report the incident to the local police and to the U.S. Attorney's office. If your first port is in a foreign country, advise the U.S. Consul and follow his directions in contacting local authority.

Should the location be within the waters of a state, then make your report to local police authority. And when the act is committed in foreign waters, the proper agency to advise is the local police force. But commonsense says give notice also to the U.S. Consul. He is your advisor and can guide you in channels free of misunderstanding and avoidable complications.

Our session in the lawyer's office is at an end. Much has been discussed, and much remains to be spoken. But we should by now have built a framework on which to place some of the details which still lie ahead. There is no such thing as a binding rule of law based on imaginary facts. The entire structure consists of actual answers settling actual problems arising from reality. So no one, ever, can state that a rule applied to the facts of Case A *must* be used in Case B. Humans possess a bewildering facility to add new twists to their dealings with each other. Yet there are discernible patterns; and they have been our targets during this inquiry. A general understanding of what those patterns involve, plus the appreciation of when to invoke professional aid, is a safe approach. By adding a liberal measure of commonsense, the boatowner should be amply armed for normal encounters.

SECTION 3

It is probably not true that Lewis Carroll found his inspiration for *Jabberwocky* after reading a policy of *marine insurance.* Yet, one cannot really be sure. Here is an excerpt from an English Lloyd's policy:

> "TOUCHING THE ADVENTURES AND PERILS WHICH WE, THE ASSURERS, ARE CONTENTED TO BEAR AND DO TAKE UPON US IN THIS VOYAGE, THEY ARE OF THE SEAS, MEN-OF-WAR, FIRE, ENEMIES, PIRATES, ROVERS, THIEVES, JETTISONS, LETTERS OF MART AND COUNTERMART, SURPRISALS, TAKINGS AT SEA, ARRESTS, RESTRAINTS, AND DETAINMENTS OF ALL KINGS, PRINCES AND PEOPLES..."

Add in such teasers as "lost or not lost," "sue and labor" or "Inchmaree," and the reactions of several courts are readily understandable. One exasperated judge labeled it "hardly intelligible"; another branded it as "absurd and incoherent."

Surely, there must be some valid reason why reasonable men so tenaciously keep using ancient and opaque words. And, indeed, there is. The aim is neither entertainment nor explanation; rather, it is certainty of interpretation. And centuries of court decisions have given each word a meaning long-shorn of ambiguity. Guided by an expert fluent in this alien tongue, we now undertake to gain a measure of comprehension from obscurity. That job, though, requires first a review of the basic principles involved, with discussion of key terminology. As with admiralty matters in general, the roots of marine insurance are imbedded in the usages of commerce. And the pleasure boatowner finds, again, that his uncomplicated needs are often served in such an unfamiliar setting. There are policies which, in some ways, seem more fitted to the pleasure mariner. But unavoidable is that boat insurance usually is tangled in the tentacles of the whole, wide marine world.

Let's start with a definition. A marine insurance policy is a CONTRACT OF INDEMNITY. As a *contract,* it is an agreement between parties by which each, for a price, gains rights and assumes responsibilities. The *indemnity* part of the definition tells much more of the story. One party agrees to protect the other against specific losses arising from maritime perils.

Now for the names given the parties. First we have the one who is protected. He is described as the ASSURED, or the INSURED. Often he is simply labeled the POLICYHOLDER. On the other side of the agreement is the one who does the protecting. He, in turn, is the ASSURER, or the INSURER. A common marine usage calls him the UNDERWRITER; and that term has an interesting history. By age-old English procedure, one who sought marine insurance would have a proposed policy circulated among the known insurers assembled at Lloyd's Coffee House on London's Lombard Street. Those insurers who chose to accept a portion of the risk would *write* their names at the bottom of the page, *under* the proposal . . . hence, the term *underwriters.* The corresponding Latin name is still sometimes used: SUBSCRIBERS. Interesting to note is that although the policy is a contract, only one side of the deal signs the written form. The policyholder's signature does not appear; only that of the underwriter is shown. The agreement of the party insured is evidenced by his payment of the required premium.

Next up for inquiry is the nature of the indemnity: against what sort of risks does the underwriter agree to protect the policyholder? The general answer is against maritime perils. This, in turn, means dangers some how resulting from the operation of the vessel. But a more careful view is necessary. There are *perils of the sea*, and not necessarily those *on* the sea. The underwriter protects against loss arising because of the extraordinary nature of risks unique to maritime operation; this need not, however, mean protection against every loss just because it is suffered *on* the sea.

Perhaps a far-fetched for instance makes the distinction. A boat, holed and sunk by an irate sawfish lunging inboard through her side, has met a peril of the sea. Suppose, though, the fish is already on board and angrily saws its way back to freedom. The resulting loss might well be outside the scope of coverage. That casualty happened on the sea, but not so clearly because of the sea. Our aim, of course, is not to catalogue each and every fine distinction. Such definition is better left to the brokers and attorneys. Even so, we should recognize that marine insurance is not a guarantee or a total protection against any and all events. It has a specific purpose of precisely defined scope. And, again, its focus is on those sea perils which cannot be guarded against by the exercise of normal human faculties. The underlying idea is indemnity against those overwhelming forces to be encountered in maritime operation. The insured need not himself be faultless; yet he cannot throw caution to the winds just because he has insurance. Gross negligence or willful misconduct can void a policy. The very sophistication of this field admits a dozen exceptions to every generalization. Nevertheless, we do well at the outset to recognize its fundamental character.

Now let's see who can be insured. Tied in with that is the reason insurance is not like Black Jack at Las Vegas. It is quite different. The underwriter does not just bet $X of protection against $Y of premium that nothing will happen. For the party insured must be sufficiently involved in the subject matter so that he actually has something to protect. He must have an INSURABLE INTEREST. *A,* in Florida, cannot buy insurance on a boat in Oregon with which he has no connection of any kind. That *would* be a sporting contract. He must have some interest to protect. Obvious examples would be a share in ownership, or a debt owed him by the Oregon boatowner. In every case, though, some shred of insurable interest is required.

A few more glances at highlights and we'll be ready to start dealing with specific clauses and terms. Back again to the subject of indemnity. How is the amount of that protection determined? There are two general approaches. One, using a VALUED POLICY, specifies at the time of agreement how much the insured vessel is worth. Then any losses are reckoned against that stipulated amount. By an UNVALUED POLICY the indemnity figure is not determined until after the loss. The actual cash value at that time is used as the basis for computation. *Yacht policies,* like marine forms in general, are customarily of the valued type. *Outboard policies* usually follow the shoreside concept, unvalued in form.

Now let's see how far we've gotten. We have a contract of indemnity written by an insurer to protect an insured against losses due to maritime perils. The maximum amount of coverage, called POLICY LIMITS, is specified in any case. The mathematics of actual payment can be based on a stipulated value of the vessel, or can be left for later determination in the light of value existing at the time of a loss.

Now we can start sifting through some specifics. There is no standard form dictated by international or government rules. Typical patterns are followed, of course; but the actual terms are not at all as uniform as a banknote. All the more necessary, then, is a careful reading of the policy. And all the more important is reliance on an informed and reputable broker. Insurers are businessmen who profit when they don't pay losses. Only rarely do they prove unable to meet obligations; but always, they must be obliged before they pay. Don't expect one paternal instinct to appear; and that is surely understandable. The policyholder has bought a certain amount of protection. He should *know* how wide is that umbrella. And he should not expect that the underwriter spell everything out for him. Read the policy; ask questions of your broker; be sure you know what is and what is not covered. No more valuable maxim can be phrased.

When one applies for marine insurance, he shoulders an unusual burden of frankness. The entire spirit of the contract presumes full knowledge beforehand of all material and relevant facts. It can be truly said that the total contract is only partially expressed in the policy. Part and parcel of the deal is opportunity for the insurer to know as much as possible about risks he will undertake; and a prime source for that data is the *application.* The courts describe the transaction as based on the utmost in good faith. Evidence of falter on the part of either party can void the agreement.

The applicant, then, starts with the viewpoint that honesty produces the best policy. He should be prepared to disclose all known facts material to the risk. Moreover, he should volunteer particulars even if he is not himself certain of their importance. Unintentional failure to disclose information known to the applicant and material to the risk can spoil the agreement. The underwriter, of course, is no naive bumpkin, unfamiliar with the game. But he is not expected to possess a detailed file on the applicant and on the boat. Yet he is being asked to protect that applicant against loss. Not at all unreasonable is it, then, to require the applicant to disclose all material facts of which he is aware.

This contract has a very significant moral flavor. The insured is the one who will actually encounter the risks; yet the underwriter will pay for resulting losses. The least to expect is fair play and the exercise of ordinary judgment in order to minimize those losses. Insurance is not a license to be heedless. The policyholder is protected against losses arising from perils peculiar to the sea. He has not bought hedges against his own dishonesty, irresponsibility or flagrant disregard of commonsense. Good faith, and good faith alone, is at the heart of the contract.

While the paperwork is being processed, a BINDER is often issued. This form would seem to be an interim binding commitment to indemnity, pending the actual issuance of the policy. And most of the time it fulfills that purpose. But it is not a policy. Many courts have dealt with parties arguing over the terms of such temporary fill-ins. They are often necessary, and they are usually trouble-free. But they are not policies. It is wise to recognize that the full terms of the contract are not really expressed until the contract itself has been issued.

We began with a sampling of the bewildering words and phrases met in some policies. And reasonable to ask is where is the code book to break down this cipher into understandable English. The answer often lies in usages of the business. What a word or phrase means. . .for example, ASSAILING THIEVES. . .is taken as what courts have specified, or what seafarers generally understand by it, or what marine insurance usage takes it to mean. And that special definition might be outside the experience of many policyholders not in everyday contact with maritime affairs. Emphasized, again, is the absolute need for expert guidance from broker or attorney in order to achieve comprehension.

Now we are ready to move in for a closer look at a yacht policy. Its basic parts are the Hull portion, the P & I clauses, the LS & HWA provisions and the medical endorsements. And as we slog along, we'll do some decoding of abbreviations. The total package of marine insurance offers protection against losses suffered by one's own property and those arising from injury or damage inflicted on others. Perhaps an apt image is to consider that what is sought is an umbrella of protection against various kinds of risks and losses. The HULL part of the coverage is designed to protect one's own property, the vessel. Let's see how the fabric of that shelter is woven.

There are two ways used to approach definition of the perils involved. By one, the NAMED PERIL POLICY, the types of danger against which protection is given are detailed in the agreement. What isn't named is not covered. By the other, the ALL RISKS POLICY, such actual expression is not so critical. But by either, exclusion clauses can be used to specify what is pushed out from under the umbrella. So don't expect *all risks* to mean what it says. At best, it means all risks except those excluded by the terms of the policy. Often, though, what is not covered by a normal form can be nudged under the umbrella, but for an extra premium.

So the hull portion of the contract covers the boat itself. When the policy is of a valued type, the amount payable on total loss is that stated in the policy. Of course, the underwriter is going to be wary of an attempt to insure a $5,000 boat for $50,000. Such over-insurance is patently suspicious and carries with it a distinct flavor of larceny in the heart. Whatever value is set can be uncomfortably binding on the underwriter; for he, by survey and inspection, has an independent opportunity to establish a figure. But even if a shady boatowner could slip an inflated value by a nodding underwriter, there might well be no profit in the deception. The insurer has several arrows left in his quiver to repel claims of over-indemnification. The very spirit of the contract finds such windfalls repugnant. *Over-valuation* and its sly shipmate, *double insurance,* have no place in our discussion. Enough to say that the game is not at all worth the candle.

Under-valuation, though, bears a closer look. Should a boat, which is reasonably worth $10,000, be insured for only $5,000, what might result? Well, in the event of a total loss, the owner would receive what he bought in protection: $5,000. Were that a partial loss, though, he finds the mathematics somewhat different. Assume the boat suffered $5,000 worth of damage. He would not receive reimbursement up to $5,000. Rather, his return would be a pro-rate based on the ratio of his insured valuation to the actual valuation. He would receive 50% compensation, because his umbrella was only 50% effective. In theory, he would be viewed as a co-insurer, retaining half the risk himself and buying protection for the other half. So he should bear half the losses. Should, instead, he have bought insurance up to the reasonable value of the boat, he would recover full reimbursement for such a partial loss. The usefulness of full-value coverage, then, is more than first meets the eye.

While we are talking of losses, we can dispose of the problem of CONSTRUCTIVE TOTAL LOSS. The term TOTAL LOSS has in mind that the boat becomes only of trifling or no value to the insured for the uses intended. A constructive total loss is one step removed. By it is meant a reduction of the boat to such a state that the cost of repair would equal or exceed its restored value. In reckoning such a loss, the British practice is more harsh than that followed under American usage. The British theory requires that, in order to reach the constructive stage, the costs of salvage and repair must equal or exceed the insured value, which is taken to be the restored value. The United States rule is more favorable to the policyholder.

It says that when salvage and repair costs exceed 50% of that repaired value, then a constructive total loss applies. Policies can specify which rule is to be followed under the contract.

The annual cost of insurance is usually reflected as a RATE or percentage based on the insured value or on the policy limits. So, a 4% rate on a $10,000 value computes to a premium of $400 per year. And the determination of that rate is controlled by quite a few individual factors. The type and condition of the boat are, of course, very important. Also involved is the area of operation, extent of communication equipment and emergency gear, and the underwriter's attitude after any prior business with the insured. Added to the credit side is evidence of competence and interest in safe operation. To that end, possession of a USCG license is an obvious plus. And active participation in the Coast Guard Auxiliary or Power Squadron can earn further advantage. Again, the tailor-made aspects of marine insurance are apparent. The degree of risk and the rate are in direct proportion.

A classic statement of coverage by the hull portion of an insurance package is:

> "...UPON THE BODY, TACKLE, APPAREL, ORDNANCE, MUNITION, ARTILLERY, BOAT AND OTHER FURNITURE, OF AND IN THE GOOD SHIP OR VESSEL CALLED THE..."

Reference to such bellicose accessories as cannon and grapeshot is on the wane; but the basic idea of insurance for the vessel and her normal fittings remains. Let's survey some of these terms to see what they mean and how they might be affected by express exclusion.

TACKLE evokes the image of anchors, spars and rigging. And that is a fair picture of what is meant. One customary provision excludes loss or damage to spars, sails and rigging while racing. The underwriter anticipates that, in the heat of competition, an owner may, like the Clipper Ship drivers of old, operate somewhat outside ordinary standards of prudence. An additional premium will be necessary to cover most of that extraordinary risk. "Most" is an important word; for usually a *spinnaker* will still be left unprotected.

Words such as APPAREL and FURNITURE seem to be as formless as a puddle of water. What really do they include, and what do they not intend to cover? The concept is to protect *the boat's* apparel and furniture, and not every article aboard. When an item is one reasonably related to boat operation, there is little question. By that standard, a barometer or a chart is clearly under cover. Stores and provisions for operation are considered protected; in fact, often they are specifically named in the clause. So, a pound of coffee and a coil of rope qualify. By contrast, a cameo brooch or a barrel of rum would appear to be excluded. One might argue that rum's medicinal and morale-building qualities should be taken into account. The persuasion of such a view is probably becalmed far back in the days of barques of oak and jolly tars. Yet, who can say? There are no rigid guidelines followed in this interpretation. When indemnity is paid for loss of a non-functional item, it might well result from additional insurance bought for the purpose. And, occasionally, recovery is had even under a standard marine policy. Sometimes, though, an underwriter's liberality in paying a minor item might be linked with as basic a practice as maintenance of good customer relationships. Better to recognize the principle, than to rely solely on recovery as a matter of right.

Incidentally, minor losses bring up the question of FRANCHISE. Marine policies can involve a *deductible provision* to screen out petty losses and the disproportionate costs of processing them. The term used to describe such a minimum is *franchise*. It can be expressed as an amount or as a percentage. In any case, it works to exclude as valid claims those losses mounting to less than the minimum. But, the pattern is not really the same as that encountered in automobile insurance. A shore policy with a $50-deductible clause says, in effect, that the policyholder pays the first $50 of loss. Should the total repair bill reach $200, then the insurer pays $150. Let's contrast a marine case. Assume that the franchise rate is 1% and that the insured value is $5,000. This means that the minimum claim must be 1% of $5,000, or $50. But it doesn't mean that the insured pays the first $50. He pays all of the loss when it is below that minimum; but he pays none of the loss when it qualifies above that amount. So, a $200 repair bill would be totally paid by the underwriter. The treatment of franchise and deductible provisions in general varies from one marine policy to another. At least, though, encounter with the strange term should not now cause confusion.

Understandably, the underwriter would prefer that the covering umbrella not reach out over the rails. He would like to restrict his risk for equipment loss to the physical limits of the boat. But here, the insured happily finds that the reach is broader. *Equipment taken off* and *stored ashore* is normally covered by the terms of a marine policy. There is, though, a limit to recovery. . . for example, 20% of the policy value.

Having side-stepped *ordnance* and *artillery,* we've now touched on *tackle, apparel* and *furniture.* What, though, about the reference to BOAT? Yacht policy usage takes this to mean a dinghy and its motor whether afloat or cradled aboard. And when such a craft is chugging along on its way to shore the umbrella of the basic hull policy, with all its terms, usually rides along.

What is left from the controlling clause is BODY. Actually, the words *hull* and *machinery* might, instead, be encountered. In any case, we now focus on the more integral parts of the vessel. During the days of pure sail, policy interpretation was much more simple for all hands. Judge, underwriter and insured, alike, could adequately fathom what was meant by the body of the vessel, and how it could be damaged by a peril of the sea. But then came the mechanical engine, with its pistons, rods, nuts and bolts. Was it part of the ship herself? Was damage caused by its failure really the result of a peril of the sea? Or was it, like the rampaging sawfish inside the ship, not to be viewed as a peril *of* the sea against which the underwriter should protect?

Matters came to a head in 1887, when England's high court, the House of Lords, reached a decision on a marine insurance case presented to test the issue. It took some research to disinter the official name of that lawsuit: Thames and Mersey Marine Insurance Company v. Hamilton. Immediate reburial is in order; for much more familiar in marine insurance as its name is INCHMAREE. Lest the uninitiated conclude that all this might refer to a diminutive performer in a carnival sideshow, we'll hasten to learn that *Inchmaree* was the name of the vessel involved. And in the lawsuit, the underwriters won out. Damage caused by an engine was not considered to result from a peril of the sea. In order to remedy this gap in the umbrella of coverage, insurance companies fashioned a special clause found in modern policies. Known more formally as the LATENT DEFECT AND NEGLIGENCE CLAUSE, it is just as often described as the INCHMAREE CLAUSE. And its importance requires that we move in for a closeup.

Here is one statement of the exact policy terms:

> "THIS INSURANCE ALSO SPECIALLY TO COVER...LOSS OF OR DAMAGE TO THE SUBJECT MATTER INSURED DIRECTLY CAUSED BY THE FOLLOWING:
>
> ACCIDENTS IN LOADING, DISCHARGING OR HANDLING CARGO OR IN BUNKERING;
>
> ACCIDENTS IN GOING ON OR OFF, OR WHILE ON DRYDOCKS, GRAVING DOCKS, WAYS, GRIDIRONS OR PONTOONS;
>
> EXPLOSIONS ON SHIPBOARD OR ELSEWHERE;
>
> BREAKDOWN OF MOTOR GENERATORS, OR OTHER ELECTRICAL MACHINERY AND ELECTRICAL CONNECTIONS THERETO, BURSTING OF BOILERS, BREAKAGE OF SHAFTS, OR ANY LATENT DEFECT IN THE MACHINERY OR HULL, (EXCLUDING THE COST AND EXPENSE OF REPLACING OR REPAIRING THE DEFECTIVE PART);
>
> CONTACT WITH AIRCRAFT OR WITH ANY LAND CONVEYANCE;
>
> NEGLIGENCE OF MASTER, CHARTERERS OTHER THAN AN ASSURED, MARINERS, ENGINEERS OR PILOTS;
>
> PROVIDED SUCH LOSS OR DAMAGE HAS NOT RESULTED FROM WANT OF DUE DILIGENCE BY THE ASSURED, THE OWNERS OR MANAGERS OF THE VESSEL, OR ANY OF THEM. MASTERS, MATES, ENGINEERS, PILOTS OR CREW NOT TO BE CONSIDERED AS PART OWNERS WITHIN THE MEANING OF THIS CLAUSE SHOULD THEY HOLD SHARES IN THE VESSEL."

More than a cure for the problem encountered by the *Inchmaree* is contained in this well-stowed stream of words and phrases. Yet what it all amounts to is probably this. The insured will be covered by the policy for losses resulting from the malfunction or negligent operation of mechanical contrivances of several sorts. And, he is protected when the loss arises from a mechanical or hull problem of which he had no knowledge, nor could have knowledge after a diligent inspection. Metal fatigue of a hidden bolt might cause the engine bed to shift and result in a torn-open side. The policyholder can expect protection when he neither knew the bolt was crystallizing, nor could have found its weakness by a reasonable, seamanlike inspection. Of course, if he had actually seen the sheared-off bolt and placed it on a list for future repairs, then he might be found wanting in due diligence.

This *Inchmaree* clause is a very, very important recital of protection valuable to pleasure boatowners, with ins and outs sometimes leading to surprises. One interesting point is the phrase "(excluding the cost and expense of replacing or repairing the defective part)." The underwriter excuses himself from paying for the sheared-off bolt which was the culprit in our example of damage. Were that energetic sawfish to have lost a tooth while gouging his way to freedom, he, to no more extent, could expect reimbursement.

What the underwriter could not reasonably be expected to pay for is loss resulting from the very nature of the object insured. The two-dollar term to describe this category is *vice propre:* an inherent vice resulting from the make-up or use of that object. So no recovery should be expected for damage due to dry rot, wear-and-tear or similar "in the nature of things" causes.

At the beginning of this chapter we met the quaint clause listing perils against which protection is to be afforded. Some of them are *of* the sea; but some of them are not. Since, though, they are named perils, they are included in the coverage. FIRE is such a named risk, and obliges the underwriter to pay for damage by the flames themselves and for consequential damage, such as resulting from chemicals or gases used to extinguish the blaze. JETTISON is another, and refers to the deliberate casting overboard of parts of the ship and contents in an attempt to relieve an emergency. THIEVES would seem to have a clear meaning. When one deliberately takes something without right, most of us would call him a thief. But the marine policy requires something else. The meaning, expressed or implied, involves ASSAILING THIEVES. The term PILFERAGE better describes sneaky stealing. What the policy has in mind is the factor of forcible entry. Of course, if the entire boat disappears, the story is different. Such a loss is a theft even if not done at gunpoint on the end of a plank jutting overboard. But when boat equipment is stolen, expect that some measure of force must be shown. In every case, the advice of a broker will help determine when something has, by policy meaning, been lost to thieves.

The classification of hostile intruders recited by the policy makes interesting reading. MEN-OF-WAR refers to belligerant acts against the insured committed by persons acting for a government under the principles of international law. What that might mean nowadays is hard to determine. At least, though, the people involved would be on official government business. LETTERS OF MART AND COUNTER-MART has in mind an old fashioned practice similar to direct governmental action. The hostile act, apparently, is not committed by official members of a government military establishment. Instead, the intruders are private interests working more or less on a commission for a government. Safe enough to say is that there are few privateers roaming the high seas in modern times. PIRATES and ROVERS seem to be the fearsome group of self-appointed assailers who operate without any sanction from any government. Surprisingly, there are still areas on the planet where such do-it-yourself interlopers are in business. SURPRISALS, TAKINGS AT SEA, ARRESTS, RESTRAINTS and DETAINMENTS refer to various hues of governmental action to stop, inspect or outright confiscate the property of the insured. Usually next to come is a phrase to mention "and all other perils." This is not a vacuum cleaner clause to sweep under the umbrella everything else in sight. Rather, it has in mind other perils of a similar kind which, by shade of meaning, were not specified in the named risks.

The war-like words encountered in the listing of named perils would seem to say that a marine policy is also a protection against *war risks*. But the umbrella shrinks by the customary addition of the *F.C. & S. clause.* FREE OF CAPTURE AND SEIZURE is the full name of the phrase; and what it does is to exclude much of what we have been talking about. The underwriter, by inserting that clause, excludes claims arising from capture, seizure, arrest, restraint, detainment, takings at sea, confiscation, requisition, and war risks in general. To the policyholder, this might seem to be a game of "gain a little, lose at least as much." As you might expect, though, there is a logical explanation. Here, again we meet a patch stitched on to an ancient policy form to plug a leak.

A similar patch is the *S.R. & C.C.* clause. It means "free of loss resulting from strikes, lockouts, labor disturbances, riots, civil commotions or the acts of any person or persons taking part in such disorder." If pickets set fire to the pier which, in turn, lights off the boat, the underwriters would consider themselves not liable for the resulting loss. Of course, by additional premium, such excluding clauses can be deleted and coverage will extend.

Included as a *named* peril is damage to the insured vessel due to collision. Now we meet the RUNNING DOWN, or *collision clause,* extending protection to claims made by others. This makes it a kind of liability insurance, obliging the underwriter for losses arising from collision with another boat. Now come the limitations. The collision must be with another boat. Fixed objects, such as piers, wharves and harbor installations, are not covered. And the entire point is to protect against *property* damage claims. Liability for personal injury or loss of life is not under this part of the umbrella. NO THIRDS OFF has an intriguing ring to it. This clause dips back to mend a tear in the umbrella of old. In earlier times, the underwriters made provision to guard against what often was an unequal result. When repairs were made to an aging vessel, the new parts were frequently far superior to the undamaged remnants. This was not indemnification in the true sense, for the insured came out of the transaction better off than before. So, the custom was to deduct one-third from the cost of repairs as an equalizing factor. Nowadays, when you see "no thirds off" in a policy, it means that no such deduction will be made. Rather, the underwriter pays for new in substitute for old. Don't expect, though, that this modern generosity is total. *Sails* and similar cloth appliances are usually paid for at their depreciated value at the time of the loss.

Now that we see the umbrella getting wider, let's mention the PRIVILEGES CLAUSE. What it does is confirm that the policy will cover while the boat is in drydock, on ways or in the shipyard. It also extends protection on trial trips, while under tow and while engaged in salvage attempts. Another inclusion is operation whether with or without a pilot.

The CONTINUATION CLAUSE can be a boon to the forgetful mariner. Not everyone keeps a reminder file to advise when such important items as insurance policies are due for renewal. This provision of the contract gives the boatowner a little leeway. In general, it recites that if the boat is at sea on the expiration of the policy, insurance continues until 24 hours after arrival at her destination, provided notice is given to the company and an additional premium is paid. But no one should be too much lulled by this stay of execution. Notification by radio to the underwriter or the broker should be given immediately. If that is not practical then give notice at some port along the way. As with everything in marine insurance, good faith and reasonable diligence upon discovery of a miscue are essential.

Yacht policies will customarily include a specification of the geographical limits of operation. These CRUISING LIMITS are to be strictly respected. The underwriter has assumed certain risks of operation within specifically described zones. Stray over the line and you are outside the umbrella. Of course, if you scurry back within the zone and there sustain a loss, coverage returns. To exceed cruising limites is not to forfeit protection altogether. Rather, it makes the boatowner his own insurance company while he is outside the pale.

Now we are ready to sail through the area of *warranties.* So strong is the requirement of good faith on the part of the insured that he will be held strictly accountable for his representations. When such a material fact is proven false, or when it is changed, the umbrella snaps shut with a resounding click. First of all, there is the matter of ownership. The underwriter doesn't just insure the boat; he really insures a particular policyholder for activities in connection with that boat. So, any change in ownership of the boat without telling the underwriter about it can void the policy. This, of course, is only fair. Otherwise, he might end up at the risk of a stranger about whom he knows nothing. . .or worse, about whose carelessness he is painfully aware.

Tied in with this *warranty of ownership* is the owner's warranty of use. Yacht policies expect that the boat will be used only for pleasure. The risk can widen instantly when the boat either carries for hire or, by charter, is turned over to strangers for operation. And the personal character of marine insurance will not stand for any such relay of control. To charter your boat is to run grave danger of voiding the contract of insurance. As we've seen in an earlier chapter, charters are risky business for boatowners.

Should you pledge the boat as security for a loan, be sure to advise the insurance company beforehand. Most of the time, this action will be required by the lender, for he will probably desire to be named on the policy as a LOSS PAYEE to be dealt with. Nonetheless, the boatowner should remember that even a pledge, not involving transfer of operating control, can affect the policy.

One more provision needs mention before we start looking at such alphabet soup as P & I and LS & HWA. Customary in policies is a SUE AND LABOR CLAUSE. It says something like this:

> "AND IN CASE OF ANY LOSS OR MISFORTUNE, IT SHALL BE LAWFUL AND NECESSARY TO AND FOR THE ASSURED...TO SUE, LABOR AND TRAVEL FOR, IN AND ABOUT THE DEFENSE, SAFE-GUARD AND RECOVERY OF THE SAID VESSEL...WITHOUT PREJUDICE TO THIS INSURANCE...TO THE CHARGES WHEREOF, THE SAID INSURANCE COMPANY WILL CONTRIBUTE ACCORDING TO THE RATE AND QUANTITY OF THE SUM HEREIN INSURED..."

At first reading, it might appear to grant to the policyholder a choice. He can help save the boat without endangering his coverage under the policy, with the underwriter promising to reimburse the expenses of his trouble; or he need not bother to try. Actually, it is far from an option. It just confirms what is an obligation of the insured: to be just as energetic as any uninsured owner in trying to preserve his boat. Having repeated that obligation, it then promises the owner that any expense for such efforts will be considered a loss covered by the terms of the policy.

Going along with that clause is another referring to the mystifying subject of GENERAL AVERAGE. Here is the idea. Suppose the boat is distressed, and the owner feels it necessary to throw overboard a heavy tackle box belonging to a guest. The jettison was for the purpose of saving the boat. In such a case, the loss of the tackle box is for the better good of all concerned. The theory, then, is that all persons involved in the problem should average out between them the cost of the things thrown overboard. In this case, that would be the value of the castaway tackle box. And by the general average clause, the underwriter agrees to pick up the tab for the insured's part of such a contribution. Incorporated in that clause is often a further agreement by the insurer. He also covers charges against the boat for salvage claims arising from troubles of the boat in distress.

Now, at last, to *P & I.* These letters refer to the seagoing equivalent of what automobile owners recognize as insurance against public liability and property damage. And, like those auto policy provisions, this part of the marine policy extends far beyond the object insured to protect the policyholder from claims against him by others who might have suffered losses by his fault.

P. & I. stands for PROTECTION AND INDEMNITY, and this umbrella goes to work in areas not reached by the hull portion of the policy. As we've seen, the running down clause of the hull provisions is the only real liability part of that section of the policy. And it limits its coverage to property damage to other vessels. P & I reaches beyond to protect against claims for personal injury and death, and for damage to structures not included in the running down clause. Covered is injury to a guest or other person on board. Also under its shelter is the cost of recovery of the boat should she sink, or its destruction if required for removal as a danger to navigation. Damage to other vessels or structures by propeller wash is protected. In addition, payment of claims by crewmembers for injury, wages, maintenance or medical care may be specified.

Sometimes the P & I portion is treated as a separate policy; but yacht useage normally incorporates it into the one contract. There are, of course, policy limits set; and deductible features are to be expected. In general, consider its operation as parallel to the familiar liability insurance available ashore.

The P & I umbrella, though, has a very important gap. It does not, by its usual terms, cover claims arising from injury or damage to persons included under the provisions of Federal Workmen's Compensation laws. So additional provisions are necessary. These are the *LS & HWA clauses;* they refer to claims under the *Longshoremen's and Harbor Workers' Act.* We need only mention the clause, for there are few noteworthy points to discuss.

A valuable endorsement to the insurance policy of a pleasure boatowner is one allowing for *medical payments* to persons injured aboard. Required are the familiar procedures of prompt notice, full reports, submission to a medical examination, and so forth. Usually excluded are claims by persons covered by compensation laws. Also not covered are trespassers, as well as those categories of persons, such as crewmembers, towards whom the boatowner has a specially outlined duty.

When a boat is not in operation, the risk shouldered by the underwriter is usually diminished. So he offers the policyholder a reduction in premium during those periods of less exposure. The procedures now met are quite regional in character. In some areas, it is the custom to store the boat ashore during certain months of the year; in others, the boat can be left afloat when *"out of season."* In all cases, though, the policyholder should stick closely to the letter of the contract. When he gains a reduction in premium because of reduced risk, he is wise to comply strictly with the terms of the policy.

Now we come to presentation of a claim when something happens. The underwriter and the broker will supply you with details of procedure; and the policy will usually spell out in terms what is required. Even so, a little commonsense discussion is in order. As soon as a casualty occurs which might be remotely connected with an insurance claim, start keeping a notebook. Such details as date, location and time are obvious. In the same category are the names and addresses of possible witnesses. Of course, the legal and moral requirements for any accident must be fulfilled. Injured parties must be treated, names and addresses exchanged, extent of injuries and damage noted. But this special notebook suggested is in addition to all that. The underwriter might be called upon to ward off some unfriendly claimants. A good memorandum of facts will be a powerful weapon in his arsenal.

Next to mention is the attitude of the insured when face to face with "the other side." The guiding rule when in contact with a potential claimant is "No Comment." Speculation on the cause of the accident is idle; in fact, it can be very worrisome to the underwriter. As soon as an accident occurs, the policyholder should adopt the stance of a reporter only, preserving the facts and nothing but the facts. . . with nary a whisper of debate.

Early in the aftermath of a casualty should be a report to your broker. The sooner the insurance company learns of the problem, the swifter be the service. Moreover, you will probably gain prompt and expert assistance in the completion of *reports* and the determination of data which might later on be crucial. Every policy states a time limit within which claims must be presented. It is inexcusable to notify the underwriter casually on the 29th day of the 11th month when the limit is one year. Always we come back to the necessity of reading the contract and relying on the broker for expert guidance. At no time will that exercise prove more worthwhile than on the occasion of a loss.

We have reached the end of a survey of the main features of a marine insurance policy. In many instances, the field is outflanked by the boatman who owns a *"homeowner's" policy* or some other form of comprehensive liability coverage. Often such insurance protects small boats within horsepower or length limits. Up to 50 horsepower or no longer than 26 feet are examples. The umbrella in such cases is of different shape and extends in quite a different manner. Its terms and conditions are more recognizable, for the pattern is really a shoreside one. In each case, the policy must be read closely to determine how it compares with the protection offered by a regular marine form. Often, its scope is adequate for small boat operation. But it is only wise to become aware of when it can serve, and of any gaps left in its shelter.

Our session with insurance is completed. Unavoidable is the conclusion that this phase of boating is a very complicated maze which can by no means be mastered by reading a few pages of summary. But that was not our aim. What we really sought was a general survey with the spotlight resting on factors of most importance. With such a background, the boatowner can best determine what he can safely handle and when he should call on his broker for guidance. Should this review only have raised a host of pertinent questions, it will have amply fulfilled its purpose.

SECTION 4

Not many of us are so affluent that we can buy a boat outright without the aid of some *financing.* So our next visit is to a bank where we will learn what is in prospect when a boatowner applies for a loan.

Pleasure boat financing is a young procedure in contrast to the well-used practices of the automobile industry. Yet already established are guidelines to mark the way. There are, of course, variations in approach between geographical areas. And in the same region, some lenders will follow routines that differ from others. But we can now define a fairly uniform course for consideration of a boat loan application.

Noteworthy at the outset is that pleasure boat loans are considered good business by many banks and lending companies. The background of experience in developing auto loan techniques, coupled with a display of sound business sense by the boating industry, has produced a favorable lending climate. The unique features of a boat loan require special consideration; for a boat is not the same as a motor vehicle. But the pattern is, in general, parallel to that encountered when financing a car. Let's follow a procedure from its initial stages to see what is involved.

Any application for credit involves factors which have been described as the three "C's" . . . *Character, Capacity* and *Collateral.* And boat loans are no exceptions. The "C" of Character establishes that the borrower is, by reputation, a person who attends to his debts in a serious and timely fashion. The second "C", Capacity, deals, not with his intentions, but with his financial ability to meet an undertaking. Sometimes, a loan officer, from his more objective point of view, can recognize what a borrower might wishfully seek to overlook. Boat owning, like many other activities, involves more expense than just purchase. Insurance, taxes, moorage and upkeep must all be reckoned with. Often the foresight of a loan officer can be of great service to nudge an applicant back towards reality on this score.

The third "C", Collateral, requires special attention in boat financing. A boat loan can be secured by the pledge of other properties, but our focus will be on the boat herself as the primary basis for security. And establishing her value for lending purposes is the first step.

The boating industry does not have such a standardized guide to values as the automobile "Blue Book". Instead, boat lenders establish *value* in two different ways. When a boat is new, the builder's selling price is often considered a sufficient key. This is particularly true when the boat is a "production" model; for its new price readily achieves a market level. The custom-built craft, though, can present a different problem, since her market value is much more unique. The procedure to appraise a used boat might then be invoked. But, generally speaking, the established selling price is a good basis for finding the loan value of a new vessel.

Used boats fall into a different category. In this field, boat lenders often rely on the *appraisal* of a professional *marine surveyor.* That is more surely the procedure for larger vessels. But when the boat is small, such an objective survey might not be required. The opinion of a reputable boat dealer or broker will often be considered sufficient.

Of interest to every owner is the schedule of *depreciation* applied to pleasure boats. We all know of very serviceable boats which far outlast any standard life expectancy. And often a vessel, like fine brandy, will increase in value with time. Additional equipment, improvements and an outstanding performance record are all factors leading to such reversals of form. Each of those cases, though, is an individual affair. What we seek is a guide to what more commonly can be expected. And such a pattern does exist. Fairly well accepted is that the useful life of a pleasure boat is about fifteen years. This is three times the life expectancy of an automobile. Fashioning a schedule of decreasing worth during that period is the next step, and here is the common practice. The first year depreciation is taken as 25 percent of the boat's original value. Then the drop is at 10 percent per year until the depreciated level is 50 percent of the starting point. Thereafter it reduces at about 5 percent per year. The first three years bear nearly half the burden of loss; and then the rate of fall drops sharply. Again, the chance of variance from this schedule is far more likely for a boat than for an automobile. To sell a three-year-old boat for comfortably near her purchase price is not rare; to sell a year-old car for within 25 percent of its new value involves canny trading.

In any case, we've progressed to the point of observing how a lender applies his three "C's" to take the measure of an applicant and boat. Balancing those three questions are another three going through the mind of the boatowner. . . how much will I get? What will it cost? How long will I have to pay it back? The answers, though, are far from standardized; for a variety of factors now come into play.

The *principal amount* of the loan should be from 75 percent to 80 percent of the value of the boat. For how long? up to seven years or even longer. What about the rate of interest? no comment. Three *general* answers are the best we can expect. Some lenders will advance a higher amount. They might be encouraged by prior lending experience in the field, or by the credit profile of the applicant. Another influence can be the participation of a boat dealer in the transaction. But such factors are unique to each situation.

So expect that a *down payment* of from 20 percent to 25 percent will be required. And the term for repayment can stretch out for quite a long time. "Up to seven years or even longer" is a wide scope. Yet, to establish a more definite estimate is impractical. Evident, at least, is that installment payments can be taylored to fit an assortment of budgets.

As for the interest rate, realism dictates "No Comment." The most that can be said is that boat loans do not fetch premium rates; rather, the price for the loan should align itself favorably with whatever levels prevail at the time of the loan.

Our applicant has by now learned the basic details of the transaction. His next concern is the legal form in which the loan will emerge. For 99.9 percent of borrowers, the writing will be more than just a promissory note without a string on one particular asset. This, of course, is no surprise. The lender will need a security agreement to complete the deal.

There are two general means in use. First is the *mortgage.* By it, the borrower signs a promissory note and then, in a mortgage agreement, secures that debt by granting to the lender certain rights in the boat. The borrower is the owner; but he turns over to the lender a lien-interest as security for the money owed. The second approach is a *conditional sales contract.* And the very name tells much of the story. The lender is, in effect, the seller. He agrees that the borrowing buyer shall have the use of the boat; and upon full payment of the contract price, title will be transferred. But until then, the lender remains legally the owner.

Which form will be used depends generally on the region and on the boat. Each mode has its advantages. The conditional sales contract gives the lender a more direct control of title; and often his power of enforcement is strengthened. Yet not always is that device preferable. Sometimes it isn't even practical.

Our discussion of general Admiralty concepts now proves worthwhile. The owner of a boat has, obviously, no priority over holders of *maritime liens.* His rights can end up subordinate to those of creditors who have such special protection. And the owner by a conditional sales contract need expect no privileged status. He, also, ranks behind maritime lien-holders. Nor is the holder of an ordinary mortgage, as we have already read, any better off. He is protected by a lien on the boat, but not by a *maritime lien.* His string on the boat is also junior to that given by Admiralty to salvors, tort claimants, crewmen, suppliers and whomever else is entitled to the powerful legal bludgeon of a maritime lien. Should a lender seek to join that select group, he would need a *preferred ship's mortgage* executed in the manner recited by the Federal Ship Mortgage Act. When discussing that form with the attorney, we learned that it is only available to vessels documented by the U.S. Coast Guard. And a requirement there is size: 5 net tons or more. The result is that lenders can only gain maritime lien security when a boat is large enough to qualify. In all other cases, such an advantage is not available.

So the preferred mortgage pattern is one reserved to larger boats. And even then it is not always required. The security is strengthened, but the rigamarole of enforcement is substantially increased. Sometimes, though, those added complications are justified. A "for instance" would be a loan on a boat that will cruise outside the United States. Then the shield of the Coast Guard document with a preferred mortgage plastered firmly on its form would be attractive. Another example would be a loan on a boat which is to be used for charter purposes. The owner might have passed muster on the Three "C's"; but the lender has no such assurances about the charterer. Yet he, as temporary owner, can have the power to create maritime liens against the boat. The lender in such cases is well-advised to insist on the PREFERRED mortgage, and with it, gain his own favorable maritime lien status. Usually, though, unless such factors exist, the complex Admiralty pattern is avoided. Instead, the lender will accept either an ordinary mortgage or a conditional sales contract.

Experience has shown that only a minority of boat loans turn sour by mixups with maritime liens. The shelter of adequate insurance extended to cover the lender usually takes care of such claims as those arising from salvage and accidents. And careful attention to the Three "C's" blunts all but stray problems on claims of suppliers.

So the normal expectation is that the lender will require execution of either a chattel mortgage or else of a conditional sales contract. And the latter form is the more common. The new boating law refers to a writing called a *security agreement.* By it the secured party can appear as legal owner. And the borrowing-buyer shows on the record as the registered owner. The pattern is, in effect, a conditional sales contract. And the method outlined by new law is made the exclusive means to show a security interest in an undocumented boat numbered under state regulations. The result is that unauthorized or undercover transfers are blocked by the requirements of recordation and of notice. For, says such a new code, no transfer of title or of any interest in such a boat shall be effective until the specified procedures are done. So the routine for most boat owners under the modern rules is quite direct. Where such customized steps are not in vogue, the owner should expect to encounter an adaptation of the ordinary security paperwork used for personal property.

No matter what the mode of expressing how security is gained, it will probably contain some clauses to offset unique Admiralty law rules. The lender will require, of course, that he be given insurance coverage. But as far as the insurance company is concerned, the primary insured party will probably be the borrower. So the lender wants to be sure that the owner has fulfilled all requirements of the policy. . .and these involve more than just timely payment of the premium. The person who buys insurance makes certain important warranties to the underwriter. And a breach of any of those warranties can void the insurance coverage for both borrower and lender. Not surprising, then, is the close attention paid by lenders to such matters. One such warranty involves *cruising limits.* The insurance can be limited to operation within a specified geographical area. To stray over the line is to become uninsured. Another refers to purpose. If the boat is warranted for private pleasure use only, then a charter can endanger protection.

What can the lender do to avoid such problems? Well, additional insurance protecting the loan amount is an excellent answer. Such, though, is not always feasible. At least there can be written into the loan agreement some limiting clauses. Standard is the promise by the pleasure boat borrower that he will not charter or lease the boat or in any way use her for hire. And not unreasonable is for the lender to require that should any warranty of the insurance policy be breached, then the total unpaid balance can immediately become payable.

No one likes to think about what might come to pass should it be necessary for a loan to be *foreclosed.* The borrower doesn't relish the thought; and neither does the lender. He is in the business of making a profit by renting his money. He is not in the used boat business. So in the great majority of cases, he will explore every reasonable alternative to enforcement of his rights under the loan agreement. In order not to cause unnecessary distress to either of them, we'll just sketch a general procedure that could be followed by a reluctant lender in protecting the outstanding balance of a loan.

Enforcing his rights under the agreement and by law, he will have the boat sold. Under the conditional sales contract, he usually is authorized to do so by following procedures spelled out in the agreement; and the filing of a court proceeding can be avoided. The mortgage form,[3] (whether ordinary or preferred), would normally require a foreclosure suit be filed in an appropriate court and then be followed by a judicial sale. In any case, the expenses of the proceedings, including a reasonable legal fee, will be first deducted from the proceeds. Then the amount remaining is applied to outstanding interest. What is left over is applied to principal. Should there still be money remaining, then the owner might get the leftovers. Of course, if there is a deficiency. . .should the loan still not be paid in full. . .then the lender can proceed against the borrower's general assets to settle the account.

Fortunately the number of foreclosures is extremely small. For, as we've already read, boat loans are usually good loans. Both boatowner and banker in the great majority of cases carry out the transaction in a fair and efficient manner. This business side of pleasure boating most often works out as a pleasant experience for everyone concerned.

Some people believe that in years to come the only place we'll see paper money will be in a museum. The modern trend, at least, is for the credit card to replace the C-Note. Of course, no one really expects to buy a yacht with a plastic charge plate. But neither will he often plunk down cash on the cabin top. Credit and financing is the rule. We've now met the high points of what lies ahead in the purchase of a boat on a time payment plan. And the prospect is not at all forbidding. It is really true that boat loans are good business, both for the boatowner and the banker, alike.

[3] *See pages 88-89*

SECTION 5

At the outset our conference-by-proxy with a customshouse broker encountered some fascinating distractions. The sleek offices, set on the mezzanine of a sizeable warehouse, look out on neatly ordered piles of bonded goods resting after voyages from all over the globe. And at rows of desks, busy clerks process shipping documents for everything from sports cars to scented candles. Typewriters and copy machines do the work of india-inked scroll. Nonetheless, here is a modern version of a 19th century Yankee trading. Goods seeking entry into our country run the gauntlet of Customs clearance side by side with export items bound for a score of foreign lands.

At such document-strewn frontiers all over the world, sovereign nations screen the ebb and flood of merchandise. For each commodity seeking entry or exit must be identified, classified and, if law requires, winnowed out of the stream. From all this we can fashion an appropriate setting for our discussion of yacht entry and clearance. A boat, even more than shipment of goods, is subject to some measure of examination as it moves from one nation's authority to another's.

Ships involved in foreign commerce accept as routine that they are aliens when they request entry into other countries. Much of the ensuing paperwork is disregarded when a pleasure boat moves in and out of foreign lands; yet we should recognize what is involved. For in the very casualness of procedure can be a somewhat risk. Whenever a pleasure boat does venture into another's preserve, it must accept submission to different rules. And sometimes we, citizens of a powerful nation, are unaccustomed to that situation.

We'll start our discussion, then, by outlining what kinds of documents could be required by a foreign power. Along the way we'll mention what actually is considered necessary. And in the process we'll gain a better concept of those elements which might well, at some time or other, assume importance.

There are three key avenues of inquiry a sovereign is inclined to pursue. One involves *identification* of persons who seek entry. Immigration and police authorities the world over have an understandable interest in the names and nationalities of travelers. Undesirables are to be kept out and fugitives are to be apprehended. So a *crew and passenger* list, supported by individual and official evidence of who the people are is a standard requirement. Local interest also dictates an examination of the health of those coming in. International cooperation to curb the spread of infectious disease demands that each country enforce some quarantine and sanitation inspection. And the third area is examination of what things are to be brought in. *Imports* subject to duty must be determined; goods otherwise dutiable which are to remain aboard must be set aside under seal. And a check of animal, agricultural and other living things capable of spreading contamination must be made. So the usual procedure involves a threefold inspection which can be described as *immigration, health* and *customs.*

Those ships seeking entry must be prepared to satisfy such local requirements. And the usual pattern involves hiring a local customs broker to do the job. He is familiar with national practices, is known to port officials, and is ready to process applications for entry with minimum fuss. The ship, in turn, must supply him with evidence to complete his task. So, she must identify herself by ownership, master, nationality and home port. Her document, issued by the government of her flag, meets that need.

In order to prove that her last port was not pest-ridden with infectious disease, she must carry a *Bill of Health.* This paper, issued by the health authorities of her last port, certifies the state of public health in that area. That assures she has not been exposed to pestilence; but what about the people aboard? Well, each person should have ready a certificate to prove that he has been innoculated during a recent period and against such diseases as international and local rules specify. And each should be prepared for a physical examination to establish that he will not be dangerous to the local population. On large vessels carrying a medical staff much of this can be handled by radio prior to arrival. But on all vessels, the likelihood of such investigation must be anticipated.

People aboard should also carry some evidence of citizenship . . . preferably in such internationally-recognized form as a passport. Its importance needs little supporting discussion. Not only does it certify to the foreign land that the holder is of a given nation; it also serves as the key to enlist the consular aid of his own country when such might be required.

Stores, supplies, baggage, personal effects and cargo . . . all these are to be listed as specified by local practice. Plants and animals should be declared so that local authority can determine their admissability. All too common, (and totally avoidable), is the distress of a person when his treasured pet faces expensive isolation or even destruction as an unacceptable entry. And the boat must stand ready to satisfy that she carries no significant amount of rodent or vermin infestation.

Much of this rigamarole stems from age-old practices to limit the spread of plague. The very word *quarantine* developed from a defense against the Black Death. *Quarante* refers to *forty;* and medieval European travelers were subject to a forty-day isolation. If they were still healthy at the end of that time, local officials felt it safe to let them in. Forty days of waiting is now history; but the word quarantine survives to designate an isolation, however brief, to determine the health of strangers.

The maritime preoccupation with rats also come from fear of the Black Death. Labeled as a carrier of bubonic plague, a rat is definitely *persona non grata* in any port. Complex procedures to discover his presence are used all over the world. A large ship carries proof of such preventive steps as fumigation or special construction to discourage rat nesting. And port officials, armed with sharp eyes and special flashlights, might stream up the gangway to search for evidence of infestation. Part of the rampart built to ward off traveling rats was the familiar ratguard. This circular shield placed around mooring lines was designed to keep the ship's rats aboard and the port's rats ashore.

The pattern for a commercial vessel is understandably extensive. Tons of Calcutta-bound grain might carry rats as stowaways. And a liner thronged with passengers and crew of a dozen nationalities will attract a close inspection. But what about a pleasure boat? How much of this international screen will be applied to a handful of people cruising into port with no more grain cargo than some boxes of dry cereal?

Requirements vary from nation to nation. And in some lands the rules seem to change from one port to another. But customary is disregard of much of the formal folderol imposed on larger craft. Nonetheless, time, place and circumstance demand that a prelude to departure on a foreign cruise be some inquiry. And the beginning point should be the consular offices in our seaport cities. There the pleasure boatman will learn specifics on documentation to be anticipated. Also valuable will be a session with a customshouse broker in one of our ports. From him can be gained many pointers on what to expect along the route. Another worthwhile source of information is the office of a shipping line trading in the areas to be visited. Added to this should be the advice of other yachtsmen who have made similar cruises. Just as prudent as a study of local charts and Sailing Directions is careful preparation of notes on the requirements of officialdom.

There is little purpose here to detail each national practice from Prince Rupert to Surinam and way points in between. The approach will vary for each region; furthermore, the requirements of the moment are subject to change with time. Of more value is a discussion of highlights, followed by those steps prudence would suggest to be ready for a wide range of circumstances.

No local official is anxious to be saddled with aliens strapped for funds. And the problem can become acute in such remote areas as the South Pacific. So not surprising is consular concern for the financial ability of visiting boatmen. Commonplace to travelers by air is the requirement that entering aliens have a roundtrip ticket assuring their ability to depart on their own resources. No less reasonable is it for some nations to be satisfied that a visiting boat will be able to supply itself for a homeward passage and not become a sort of public ward.

If any fishing it to be done in foreign areas, the time to find out about licenses is before departure. Mexico, for example, requires that the boat and those aboard be separately licensed for sport fishing in national waters.

A large measure of reciprocity exists between the United States and nearby British-oriented areas. The usual pattern involves little more than a report to officials at the port of entry and the acquisition of a *cruising permit* for the region. Then, upon departure, one presents himself to officials at the last port and receives their Bon Voyage. Moreover, expect that no fees will be charged. This is the procedure in Canada and throughout much of the formerly British West Indian area.

Cruising in waters of Central American countries might well be less certain in procedures. Some owners have commented that on occasion there seems to be no pattern at all. The paperwork and attendant fees in one port might be no burden; but the requirements a few miles down the same nation's coast might be quite different. There would often appear to be sufficient local control in the office of port authorities to produce widely varying practices. Personality, lingual ability, day and time of appearance can all be factors. Realism demands that one recognize the casual manners in remote ports all over the world. And Central America has its share of such tranquil locations. This is not to say there are no regulations. Rather, it suggests that interpretation and manner of enforcement might well be random.

A Caribbean passage can run the gamut from perfunctory steps in British areas to much more formal requirements in Colombia and Venezuela. Again, careful inquiry beforehand is indicated. And in any area, affiliation with an American yacht club can be of value. A pennant whipping smartly aloft has served as an effective introduction to fellow yachtsmen in many a strange area. And with that introduction can come priceless assistance in compliance with local requirements.

But more than an indexed notebook beneath a club burgee is needed to provide sensibly for what might occur. Persons aboard can suffer illness and require treatment ashore away from a local port. It might prove necessary for someone to return home by another means than the boat. Some positive evidence of nationality should be carried . . . and a passport is hard to beat. Even if the foreign land requires no visa, it is always good practice for each person to carry a valid passport. The fees are nominal; and the protection is well worthwhile.

A call to the U.S. Public Health Service in an American port can provide data on the innoculation requirements of countries to be visited. Each person should have an internationally-accepted record of immunizations received.

Sometimes confusion develops over re-entry into the United States with foreign made equipment such as cameras, binoculars, radios, tape recorders and the like. A wise precaution before departure is to register such articles with the U.S. Customs. Then there should be no suggestion upon re-entry that the items are subject to import regulations.

Pleasure boats should have little concern with a bill of health required, as we've seen, of commercial craft. Rare is an inquiry by a second port of call regarding health conditions at an earlier one visited by a yacht. Clearance papers issued by a Port Captain or other official in ordinary course of business will usually suffice. Even so, knowledge that such a document exists might be useful as valuable forewarning.

Incidentally, here is a comment worthy of note. Throughout the world there still lingers a deference to impressive paperwork liberally sprinkled with official-looking labels. In the United States we nowadays seldom encounter documents with colofrul ribbons trailing in the wake of gold stickers and thick wax seals. So we cannot expect to dazzle a local port official with any such display. But don't belittle the impact of form in some areas. If you have a choice between a nononsense paper and one more elaborate in appearance, choose the latter. Someplace along your route it might bring an unexpected advantage.

In the same vein is the matter of multiple copies. We are not alone in fathom-long distribution lists requiring echoes and encores to a dozen desks. The practice seems to be an international malady. Whenever possible, acquire duplicates of key documents. Photocopies are not always acceptable; yet they are certainly better than none at all. Fending off the insistence of a local official for your one-and-only copy of a particular paper can become annoying.

Now to our last topic of discussion. How does the boat identify herself? What paperwork is involved to establish in a foreign port that she is entitled to the courtesies extended to U.S. Nationals and to their property? This brings us to the subject of *documentation.*

To begin with, a boat is an item of personal property, as is a pair of shoes. We barely stop to think about the nationality of crepesoled sneakers. Pressed for an answer, we would probably conclude they carry the flag of their owner. In theory the boat is no different. She also could be viewed as bearing the citizenship of her owner. But she is, in fact, much more personified than a pair of shoes. As a result there exists a very definite need to evidence her ownership and nationality by some sort of writing.

Within the United States, the purpose is achieved by several alternative means. Both State registration practices and the documentation procedures administered by the U.S. Coast Guard can do the job. To discuss which is more desirable within our own boundaries is to start a lively, but probably not important, debate. In earlier chapters we've read that when a boat is to be mortgaged, the Coast Guard document can become essential. And should the vessel be traveling regularly between states, her exemption as a documented boat from state procedures might be helpful. Not true, though, is that the federal identification saves her from local taxation. The revenue net is closely woven, and no freedom from a tax collector can be expected. In fact, interstate exchange of data on registered boats is reaching such levels of efficiency that the web to bag personal property, sales and use tax assessments is fashioned of very fine mesh.

Of no greater force is the supposed advantage that only a Coast Guard-documented boat is entitled to fly the national ensign. No matter how official might be such a distinction, little heed is shown in practice. No more than purchase at a marine supply house seems to be the actual prerequisite.

The major advantage of the Coast Guard procedure, other than in mortgage situations, might well lie in the area of a foreign voyage. For the station and grandeur of an instrument prepared by the national government does outshine the testimonial of one of its member states.

In order to give public notice that a private vessel is of U.S. ownership and entitled to the protection afforded the flag by our government, federal law specifies three general patterns to be followed. One results in the issuance of a *Certificate of Registry.*[4] By it the world is told that the U.S.-owned ship intents to engage in lawful foreign commerce, and that the Marine Corps-backed State Department stands ready to insure her safe conduct. This kind of document is not for pleasure craft. By another procedure the ship can be certified as *enrolled* on the records of U.S.-owned vessels, with the intention that her use be more restricted to domestic waters.

The third method results in a *license*. By it, citizenship is certified and the category of her intended use is detailed. Here is the type document a foreign-going pleasure boat might use: the *License of Yacht.*[5] She is identified as U.S.-owned; she carries the flag by right; and both diplomats and Leathernecks can be summoned to her aid. Of course the same powerful support is available to any citizen and his boat, documented or not. But the affiliation is somehow more evident when the instrument bears the national mark.

The steps a boat follows to acquire such a paper[6] are detailed and time-consuming. Administration is by the Officer-in-Charge, Marine Inspection, of the Coast Guard District of her home port. And there are some unavoidable preliminaries to eligibility.

First of all, the boat must be totally owned by U.S. citizens. In legal terms there are two kinds of people: a natural person is of the flesh-and-blood variety; an artificial person is a corporation. Each natural person who participates in ownership of a U.S.-documented boat must be a citizen. Should there be 3 or 30, each possessing a piece of ownership, they must all be citizens. Current practice requires that foreign-born citizens must personally present at the Coast Guard Office their evidence of naturalization. If the owner is a corporation, then it must be a U.S. corporation. And no more than 25 percent of the control of that entity can be vested directly or indirectly in aliens.

A second barrier to be hurdled is size. The boat must measure to 5 net tons or more. And here we encounter a quaint but confusing facet of things maritime. There are tons and then, again, there are tons. A long ton is 2,240 pounds; a metric ton is 2,204 pounds; a short ton is 2,000 pounds. But a measurement ton isn't any of them. For it speaks, not of weight, but of volume. Stemming from dusty antiquity, the same word, *ton* is used in maritime parlance sometimes to describe weight and sometimes, volume. For documentation purposes it speaks of measured volume. And the unit of

[4] *See pages 90-91* [5] *See page 86* [6] *See page 97*

1 ton represents 100 cubic feet. So, 5 net tons is really saying 500 cubic feet.

Let's pursue this tonnage business just a bit more so that, once and for all, we can lay it and its quirks by the heels. In doing so, we risk delving into subjects having scant relevance to pleasure boating. Yet, a clear understanding of the basis for pleasure boat measurement should make the excursion worthwhile.

In general, weight measurements of a vessel are described by such terms as *displacement* tonnage and *deadweight* tonnage. The unit is the long ton; and the labels are usually restricted to commercial vessels. Displacement speaks of the total weight of the ship and all her contents. Deadweight refers to the weight of the contents only: Fuel, water, stores and any cargo.

When the internal volume of a ship is measured, the unit is, as we've seen, 100 cubic feet per ton. And there are two volume tonnages. *Gross* refers to the total enclosed volume, subject to specified exemptions. *Net* refers to a measure of less extensive internal areas. For a commercial vessel, it generally describes the areas available for the carriage of cargo.

The bewildering result can be this set of tonnage statistics for a large ship: Displacement, 15,000; Deadweight, 10,000; Gross, 8,000; Net, 4,500. Translated, this means that she and her contents can weigh 15,000 long tons. Of that amount, 10,000 long tons is deadweight contents. Measurement of her enclosed spaces amounts to 800,000 cubic feet. Reduced to units of 100 cubic feet, this produces 8,000 Gross tons. And of that, 450,000 cubic feet (or, 4,500 Net tons) are useful for revenue. During sea wars, widely varying claims of shipping losses might now be understandable. The enemy who sinks the ship we describe could honestly advertise a 15,000 ton victory; yet his opponent could just as truly claim only a 4,500 ton loss.

Having straightened out the tonnage tangle, let's get back to pleasure boat admeasurement. The minimum requirement is a measure of 5 net tons, or 500 cubic feet of internal space. And determination of the actual amount can be done two ways. By application to the local Coast Guard Officer in Charge, Marine Inspection, appointment can be made for a formal physical measurement. After reference to steel tape and plans, the measuring officer will go through a formula and produce the new tonnage. More attractive, though, is a simplified procedure. The owner himself wields the yardstick to establish the key dimensions. Let's see what is involved.

Three dimensions are needed; and they are expressed either in feet and inches, or in feet and decimal parts of a foot. First to be found is the *overall length*, and here is the official definition of the measure:

> "THE HORIZONTAL DISTANCE BETWEEN THE FOREMOST PART OF THE STEM AND THE AFTERMOST PART OF THE STERN, EXCLUDING BOWSPRITS, BUMPKINS, RUDDERS, OUTBOARD MOTOR BRACKETS, AND SIMILAR FITTINGS OR ATTACHMENTS."

At the risk of appearing country bumpkinly, we should now ask, "What is a bumpkin?" It's a boom or bracket projecting from the hull and to which some sail control device such as a tack or brace is secured. Next comes the *overall breadth,* detailed officially this way:

> "THE HORIZONTAL DISTANCE, EXCLUDING RUB RAILS, FROM THE OUTSIDE OF THE SKIN (OUTSIDE PLANKING OR PLATING) ON ONE SIDE TO THE OUTSIDE OF THE SKIN ON THE OTHER, TAKEN AT THE WIDEST PART OF THE HULL."

and the third is *overall depth,* described as:

> "THE VERTICAL DISTANCE TAKEN AT OR NEAR MIDSHIPS FROM A LINE DRAWN HORIZONTALLY THROUGH THE UPPERMOST EDGES OF THE SKIN AT THE SIDES OF THE HULL (EXCLUDING CAP RAIL AND TRUNKS, CABINS, OR DECKHOUSES) TO THE OUTBOARD FACE OF THE BOTTOM SKIN OF THE HULL. THIS EXCLUDES THE KEEL UNLESS THE KEEL IS COVERED BY THE SKIN."

When a boat is designed for sailing, the overall length and depth are measured in the vertical plane of the centerline; and the overall breadth is measured in a line at right angles to that plane. *Designed for sailing* officially refers to a boat, whether or not equipped with an auxiliary motor, which has the fine lines of a sailing craft and is in fact propelled by sail or capable of so being propelled, other than by a mere steadying sail.

Now the applicant multiplies the three dimensions together to establish a volume factor in cubic feet. This product is called LBD. If the boat is designed for sailing, her *gross tonnage* is taken as 1/2 (LBD/100). If not designed for sailing, her gross is 2/3 (LBD/100). For multi-hull vessels, the gross is reckoned as the sum of the tonnages of the hulls. And for houseboats and similar craft whose deckhouses are exceptionally large, the volume of the deckhouse (expressed in the 100-cubic foot ton units) is added to that of the hull.

With gross tonnage in hand, the owner now calculates the *net tonnage* this way: When a boat is designed for sailing, net equals nine-tenths of the gross tonnage: 0.9 x gross = net. When a boat is not designed for sailing, net equals eight-tenths of the gross tonnage: 0.8 x gross = net. For a boat which has no propelling machinery inside her hull, net equals gross.

The mathematically-inclined can have a field day reducing these several steps into one formula. For example, the non-sailing boat routine seems to reduce to about this: 0.00533 x LBD = net tonnage. And the sailing formula shrinks to 0.0045 x LBD. Here are some examples, following the trail step-by-step. And the dimensions mentioned are not those of any particular boat. They are selected as more-or-less reasonable and just for purposes of seeing the pattern.

First, let's measure an inboard powerboat. The overall length is taken as 40 feet. Her overall beam is 12 feet, and her overall depth is 9 feet. We seek her net tonnage. Here is the way we would reach an answer:

40 x 12 x 9 = 4,320 cubic feet
2/3 x 4,320 = 2,880 cubic feet
2,880/100 = 28.8 gross tons
28.8 x 0.8 = 23.04 net tons

Do it by the unofficial short-cut method and you find:

net tonnage = 0.00533 x LBD
net tonnage = 0.00533 x 40 x 12 x 9
net tonnage = 23.0256 tons

Here is an example of an auxiliary sloop. She measures 27 feet overall, with a 9-foot beam and an overall depth of 7 feet to her skin-covered keel. What is her net tonnage?

27 x 9 x 7 = 1,701 cubic feet
1/2 x 1701 = 850.5 cubic feet
850.5/100 = 8.505 gross tons
8.505 x 0.9 = 7.6545 net tons

The short-cut says net tonnage = 0.0045 x LBD. This produces: 0.0045 x 27 x 9 x 7, or the same 7.6545 net tons. Both of these boats would qualify for documentation.

But what about an inboard that is 22 feet long, 7 feet in breadth and 6 feet in overall depth?

22 x 7 x 6 = 924 cubic feet
2/3 x 924 = 616 cubic feet
616/100 = 6.16 gross tons
6.16 x 0.8 = 4.928 net tons

The factor method would bring this answer:

net tonnage = 0.00533 x 22 x 7 x 6
net tonnage = 4.92492

In either case, the boat would seem to fall just short of the mark, unless her owner made artful use of a rubber ruler. Answers are not going to be carried out to several decimal places; the normal practice is to round off to the nearest tenth. But the Coast Guard does caution that if the tonnage computed by the simplified method[7] falls short of 5 net, it is not likely that formal admeasurement will do any better.

Bobbing astern now is the mathematics session. What next will the owner encounter in his pursuit of documentation? Well, he must establish a chain of ownership from the building of the vessel to the date of application. The starting point is a paper called the *Master Carpenter's Certificate.*[8] This is the boatbuilder's certification of time, place and details of construction. Analogous to the doctor's statement regarding a birth, it certifies to the circumstances of the birth of the boat. And the pursuit of

[7] *See pages 92-93* [8] *See page 95*

that statement can sometimes become a major task. As time goes on, boats move from one area to another and boatyards go into and out of business. Yet the Master Carpenter's Certificate must be presented for documentation. A buyer, then, who harbors even a remote inclination to document his boat should anticipate this requirement and, if possible, have it passed along to him by the seller. When a foreign boat is to be documented, the Coast Guard shows some mercy. Instead of precipitating an international manhunt for a foreign builder, they will accept the last document issued by the foreign government under which the boat held a previous document.

The chain of title from Birth to Now can prove equally tedious. Required is her history, documented by evidence of transfers along the way. State registration records are acceptable; foreign title abstracts will serve. Sometimes, though, the applicant spends time pouring over telephone books and other address lists to find leads. One advantage of purchase at an Admiralty court sale is that the chain from there back is severed. The vessel is then reborn; and the need for further certification dates from then forward.

The owner has measured the boat, assembled the supporting evidence to establish a chain of title, and still has reserves of energy to complete the job. What, then, is next? A documented vessel has a *home port*[9] and a *hailing port.* Her owner now addresses himself to their selection.

The home port is that one which is at or closest to the business address of the vessel. For a yacht, it amounts to the port at or closest to the home of the owner. When more than one owner is involved then the location of the managing owner is the key.

The Coast Guard, however, has not designated every inlet as a Home Port. So the range of selection is not without limits. What it all amounts to is that the residence of the owner places him within a *Home Port Designation Zone.* At the Coast Guard office in that home port, the boat's documentation file will be processed and kept. The owner, then, has little actual latitude in the selection of home port. And one of the reasons for the constrictions is the matter of taxation. Some owners, seeking favorable tax rates and procedures, try to document their boats in out-of-the-way places where, perhaps, the local assessments for schools and street lights are minimal. More and more, cooperation between Coast Guard officials and local tax collectors is defeating such maneuvers. Expect that there will be some inquiry . . . perhaps even an actual investigation . . . to determine if the applicant does, in truth, maintain a residence in the home port zone. And once such a designation is made, do not expect that it can be changed at will. For then the question of why arises. Assurance that the purpose is not avoidance of taxation or liens might well be required.

Identification of residence by reciting a post office box number will probably not be accepted without explanation. Those boaters who live aboard have a valid reason for the use of such a mailing address. But when one's bedstead rests on solid earth, more than a postal number will be needed.

Selection of the boat's *hailing* port is less restricted. It must be a location within the home port zone; but beyond that requirement, the

[9] *See page 96*

owner is not held to a tight rein. In fact, some of the results can be humorous. An owner, for example, who resides in the lofty Rockies at Aspen, Colorado, would be within the home port zone of St. Louis, Missouri. Since his regal 70-foot cruiser is not equipped with skis, he keeps her berthed at Southern California's Marina del Rey. What might be the story on her home and hailing ports? The home port would be St. Louis, Missouri, for the owner resides within its zone. As for hailing, he could use St. Louis or Aspen. So should the stern of a coastal pleasure boat display such a name as Aspen or Gila Bend or Santa Fe, don't despair that the days of Noah are returning. Rather, suspect her owner, in his land-locked residence, elected to bestow on her a very unique distinction.

Quite evident is that the goal of documentation is not to be reached by an afternoon visit to a Coast Guard office. Several weeks, at least, will pass before the job is done. And the requirements of citizenship and size are unalterable conditions for eligibility. When a vessel does not qualify, she is not, of course, barred from foreign cruising. Many owners of smaller vessels have voyaged abroad with no tremor of difficulty arising from lack of a document. Yet, if it can be acquired, the foreign-bound owner is probably better off by undertaking the lengthy procedures to get it in hand.

We'll conclude with a word about transfer of boats from U.S. flag to foreign registry and the reverse procedure to document an alien vessel. The international practice is to respect the interest of each sovereign in the disposition of vessels entitled to fly its flag. Before a U.S.-flag boat over 65 feet long can be passed along to foreign ownership, the permission of the U.S. Maritime Administration must first be procured. This step allows our government to inquire about outstanding taxes, liens, duties, the possible detriment to national security by a sale to unfriendly interests, and the general propriety of the transfer. Viewed the other way, our government respects the concern of other countries when a boat of another flag requests U.S. documentation.[10] Evidence that the foreign government approves of such a transfer will usually be required. *Comity* is a word to describe the international practice of, "Scratch my back and I'll scratch yours." By the exchange of such courtesies, countries throughout the world discourage attempts to avoid legal obligations.

We've reached the end of our discussion of entry, clearance and documentation. Each chapter of our survey confirms that no specific details can reasonably be defined on these pages. Emphasized, though, is that no such precision should be expected. Each element of the legal side of boating involves such technicality that the aid of specialists is often required. We seek the outlines only; and if they have been spelled out, then our mission has been accomplished.

[10] *See page 94*

SECTION 6

In readying Cleopatra's barge for a pleasure cruise, little heed was probably given to such niceties as B-II fire extinguishers, Personal Flotation Devices or the construction and character of her sidelights. Times, though, have changed. A modern pleasure boat would receive Marc Antony aboard after much more attention to safe navigation. And the measure of required safety grows more precise as time goes on.

All government control of private seafaring is for the purpose of serving the public interest. And for many years the scope of that interest was quite limited. Not much general concern was found in the recreational use by a citizen of the sovereign-less High Seas. Whether his operation was safe or sorry appeared hardly to be the business of anyone but himself and those who chose to keep him company.

Of course, the matter of signals to be given and maneuvers to be made could affect others; so International Rules of the Road introduced some restraints. And a new set of such rules is due in 1976. But, by and large there were not many ocean-going fetters. When, though, national waters were involved, more demanding requirements seemed reasonable. So for many years specific rules have existed regarding minimum equipment, speed limits, clearance of channels, aids to navigation...and even pollution. Nonetheless, the extent of restraint on recreational craft was minimal.

Now the picture is changing. Millions of pleasure boats make use of coastal and inland waterways. And with that population explosion has come a reassessment of what is in the public interest. One result is the *Federal Boat Safety Act of 1971.* Its initial impact is on construction, safe boating programs and vessel identification. But the foundation has been laid for much wider supervision. This comprehensive law points the way to detailed government control of what yachtsmen have grown to accept as a last frontier of freedom.

To debate whether the development is good or bad is to mix idle chatter and nostalgia. The law is here and it is being implemented. Cattlemen are said to have bitterly decried the advent of fences on the western prairies a century ago. Twentieth century yachtsmen should evidence a more knowledgeable outlook. On these pages we will accept this new law as a legal reality emerging from Congress after a review of statistics and studies. Our aim is to survey what it presages and how it fits in the scheme of modern boating.

Lengthy quotation of law is often not too informative. But we might find a focus for this new act in its **Declaration of Policy and Purpose:**

> "SEC.2. IT IS HEREBY DECLARED TO BE THE POLICY OF CONGRESS AND THE PURPOSE OF THIS ACT TO IMPROVE BOATING SAFETY AND TO FOSTER GREATER DEVELOPMENT, USE AND ENJOYMENT OF ALL THE WATERS OF THE UNITED STATES BY ENCOURAGING AND ASSISTING PARTICIPATION BY THE SEVERAL STATES, THE BOATING INDUSTRY, AND THE BOATING PUBLIC IN DEVELOPMENT OF MORE COMPREHENSIVE BOATING SAFETY PROGRAMS; BY AUTHORIZING THE ESTABLISHMENT OF NATIONAL CONSTRUCTION AND PERFORMANCE STANDARDS FOR BOATS AND ASSOCIATED EQUIPMENT; AND BY CREATING MORE FLEXIBLE REGULATORY AUTHORITY CONCERNING THE USE OF BOATS AND EQUIPMENT. IT IS FURTHER DECLARED TO BE THE POLICY OF CONGRESS TO ENCOURAGE GREATER AND CONTINUING UNIFORMITY OF BOATING LAWS AND REGULATIONS AS AMONG THE SEVERAL STATES AND THE FEDERAL GOVERNMENT, A HIGHER DEGREE OF RECIPROCITY AND COMITY AMONG THE SEVERAL JURISDICTIONS, AND CLOSER COOPERATION AND ASSISTANCE BETWEEN THE FEDERAL GOVERNMENT AND THE SEVERAL STATES IN DEVELOPING, ADMINISTERING AND ENFORCING FEDERAL AND STATE LAWS AND REGULATIONS PERTAINING TO BOATING SAFETY."

Its **Definitions** section defines a **boat** as

> "SEC.3.(1)"BOAT MEANS ANY VESSEL
> A) MANUFACTURED OR USED PRIMARILY FOR NONCOMMERCIAL USE; OR
> B) LEASED, RENTED OR CHARTERED TO ANOTHER FOR THE

LATTER'S NONCOMMERCIAL USE; OR
C) ENGAGED IN THE CARRYING OF SIX OR FEWER PASSENGERS."

A **vessel** is described as

"SEC.3.(2)...EVERY DESCRIPTION OF WATERCRAFT, OTHER THAN A SEAPLANE ON THE WATER, USED OR CAPABLE OF BEING USED AS A MEANS OF TRANSPORTATION ON THE WATER."

"SEC.3.(5)...EVERY PERSON CARRIED ON BOARD A VESSEL OTHER THAN
A) THE OWNER OR HIS REPRESENTATIVE;
B) THE OPERATOR;
C) BONA FIDE MEMBERS OF THE CREW ENGAGED IN THE BUSINESS OF THE VESSEL WHO HAVE CONTRIBUTED NO CONSIDERATION FOR THEIR CARRIAGE AND WHO ARE PAID FOR THEIR SERVICES;
OR
D) ANY GUEST ON BOARD A VESSEL WHICH IS BEING USED EXCLUSIVELY FOR PLEASURE PURPOSES WHO HAS NOT CONTRIBUTED ANY CONSIDERATION, DIRECTLY OR INDIRECTLY, FOR HIS CARRIAGE."

And **associated equipment** is detailed as

"SEC.3.(8)...
A) ANY SYSTEM, PART OR COMPONENT OF A BOAT AS ORIGINALLY MANUFACTURERED OR ANY SIMILAR PART OR COMPONENT MANUFACTURED OR SOLD FOR REPLACEMENT, REPAIR, OR IMPROVEMENT OF SUCH SYSTEM, PART OF COMPONENT;
B) ANY ACCESSORY OR EQUIPMENT FOR, OR APPURTENANCE TO, A BOAT;
AND
C) ANY MARINE SAFETY ARTICLE, ACCESSORY, OR EQUIPMENT INTENDED FOR USE BY A PERSON ON BOARD A BOAT;
BUT
D) EXCLUDING RADIO EQUIPMENT."

Applicability of the law is specified in these words:

"SEC.4.(A) THIS ACT APPLIES TO VESSELS AND ASSOCIATED EQUIPMENT USED, TO BE USED, OR CARRIED IN VESSELS USED, ON WATERS SUBJECT TO THE JURISDICTION OF THE UNITED STATES AND ON THE HIGH SEAS BEYOND THE TERRITORIAL SEAS FOR VESSELS OWNED IN THE UNITED STATES."

"SEC. 4. (C) THIS ACT, EXCEPT THOSE SECTIONS WHERE THE CONTENT EXPRESSLY INDICATES OTHERWISE, DOES NOT APPLY TO -
1) FOREIGN VESSELS TEMPORARILY USING WATERS SUBJECT TO UNITED STATES JURISDICTION;
2) MILITARY OR PUBLIC VESSELS OF THE UNITED STATES, EXCEPT RECREATIONAL-TYPE PUBLIC VESSELS;
3) A VESSEL WHOSE OWNER IS A STATE OR SUBDIVISION THEREOF, WHICH IS USED PRINCIPALLY FOR GOVERNMENTAL PURPOSES, AND WHICH IS CLEARLY IDENTIFIABLE AS SUCH;
4) SHIPS' LIFEBOATS."

Next following in the Act are sections which spell out the power of the Coast Guard to establish and enforce standards of manufacture. Provision for labels evidencing compliance, for exemptions and for prohibitions are then recited. Steps are also outlined to effect buyer protection by requiring that a manufacturer give notice of defects and of procedures for correction at his expense. To encourage compliance, quite severe civil penalties and provisions for restraint by court injunction are included.

A reading of the first part of this law gives ample evidence of one aim. Placed squarely in the light of public concern has been regulation of manufacture to assure that safe equipment will be used on our national waters and by our citizens when on the High Seas.

But safety in construction and design is only part of the story. The Act also provides for criminal penalties should a vessel be *operated* in violation of the new law. Repeated is the Coast Guard power to determine by on-board inspection if a boat is hazardous; and, if so, the power to order a return to moorings until the condition is remedied. In case of a collision, accident or casualty, the operators involved are required to assist each other as best they can in the circumstances. And an exchange of name, address and vessel identification is specified. This responsibility of operation is not new; it has just been widened. But then comes a *"Good Samaritan"* clause to relieve the concern of those who render aid in good faith but not with skill. The exact wording is this:

"SEC.16(B) ANY PERSON WHO COMPLIES WITH SUB-SECTION (A) OF THIS SECTION OR WHO GRATUITOUSLY AND IN GOOD FAITH RENDERS ASSISTANCE AT THE SCENE OF A VESSEL COLLISION, ACCIDENT, OR OTHER CASUALTY WITHOUT OBJECTION OF ANY PERSON ASSISTED, SHALL NOT BE HELD LIABLE FOR ANY CIVIL DAMAGES AS A RESULT OF THE RENDERING OF ASSISTANCE OR FOR ANY ACT OF OMISSION IN PROVIDING OR ARRANGING SALVAGE, TOWAGE, MEDICAL TREATMENT, OR OTHER ASSISTANCE WHERE THE ASSISTING PERSON ACTS AS AN ORDINARY, REASONABLY PRUDENT MAN WOULD HAVE ACTED UNDER THE SAME OR SIMILAR CIRCUMSTANCES."

Public interest expands another league...and reasonably so. Not only should those directly involved in a casualty be required to give aid; there should be no damper put on the inclination of anyone around to give a helping hand. An impediment has been the possibility of unwitting involvement in a lawsuit. Section 16(b) seems to allay such bystander fears.

The next sections of the Act outline a national *numbering system* for vessels. The aim is to achieve a standard pattern throughout the country, and one keyed to a more uniform program of safe boating. Each state can handle administration within its region; if it does not, then the Coast Guard handles the job.

The last portions of the law describe the establishment and operation of state boating safety programs, with provision for consultation, cooperation and Federal funding.

There is the skeleton for more comprehensive national supervision of boating with quite a few chunks of meat already in place on the bones. To carry out this pattern will require many new regulations, of course. Congressional law tends to set out broad outlines and then delegate authority to an agency to fill in the details. The Coast Guard will do so under this law by its own edicts and by participating with State agencies in the development of local rules. It will take some time for all this to come to pass; yet already new regulations are beginning to appear. Until they do, though, fragments of earlier laws remain in effect. So the present scene is a mixture of old and new.

First receiving attention seems to be the subject of manufacture. Then to follow will be recasting of operational requirements. Of course, the new Act is no totally-exclusive blanket intended to supplant all laws applicable to boating. The various sets of Rules of the Road will still be in force; and the main body of Admiralty will apply as appropriate. Moreover, side by side will appear other rules designed to meet our complicated modern life. An example is regulation designed to promote environmental protection.

It is too early in the game to prophecy specifically what will be the duties and responsibilities of the boatowner. In fact, the sensible approach is for us to emphasize, not so much the details, but rather the avenues at hand to learn details.

In regular fashion, changes are proposed, discussed and sometimes turned into law. To see what this can involve, let's take a quick look at the matter of a marine sanitation device. In order to carry out the purpose of the *Federal Water Pollution Control Act*, regulations were proposed to require installation of some sort of sewage handling system aboard small craft. One approach was to specify a treatment device which would accept waste matter and render it safe for discharge into the waterways. The other approach was to require that boats carry a holding receptacle to retain sewage safely aboard for later transfer ashore. At first what seemed to be in store was a high-performance appliance to convert waste into harmless material suitable for overboard discharge. But a second look at the technology involved suggested the target as presently unrealistic for small craft. So, the upshot has been a modification of aim. The **Environmental Protection Agency** has issued a standard requiring no overboard discharge of waste. This would seem to mean the need for holding tanks. Provided, though, is that boatowners who, prior to the effective date of standards, have a device aboard suitable for primary treatment and disinfection, will be viewed as in compliance for a period of time after that date. The Coast Guard, in turn, has the task of setting up rules consistent with **EPA** standards. And that, in a new field, is a demanding job. the public must be protected, but the means must still be practical. The holding tank approach, specified by the **EPA**, seems to be the basic answer. But recognized also is that the technology of waste treatment might well make possible some other alternatives. To that end, the Coast Guard has invited comment on the design and construction of feasible devices, as well as on procedures for testing and certification.

The point of the story is clearly made. The boatowner should anticipate an increase in regulation on many fronts, including some that are just emerging from the development stage. And he must keep himself informed of such changes as they appear.

Here, then, is a reasonable way to keep in touch. Periodically contact the Office of Boating Safety at District Coast Guard headquarters in your region. One of its prime functions is to keep the boating public advised on existing regulations and on those just over the horizon. Your local office of the Federal Communications Commission has data on requirements for radio equipment. And your state boating agency will have available information on local requirements. High on the list of information sources are both the Coast Guard Auxiliary units and those of the U.S. Power Squadron in your area. And boating magazines regularly carry informative articles outlining what has come to pass. This part of boating is in such transition that frequent updating is very much in order.

Understandable is a measure of hesitation before any recap of what presently might be officially required of a pleasure craft under this new Act. For typewriters are busy from Washington to Honolulu recasting the tangled threads from several sets of laws into a more unified form. Here, though, is a recast of a minimum equipment schedule presented by the Coast Guard in its pamphlet, **Pleasure Craft...Federal Requirements for Boats, (CG-290:**

MINIMUM REQUIRED EQUIPMENT BY LENGTH OF BOAT

1. LESS THAN 16 FEET IN LENGTH:

BACK-FIRE FLAME ARRESTER- ONE APPROVED DEVICE ON EACH CARBURETOR OF ALL GASOLINE ENGINES INSTALLED AFTER APRIL 25, 1940 EXCEPT OUTBOARD MOTORS.

VENTILATION- AT LEAST TWO VENTILATOR DUCTS FITTED WITH COWLS OR THEIR EQUIVALENT FOR THE PURPOSE OF PROPERLY AND EFFICIENTLY VENTILATING THE BILGES OF EVERY ENGINE AND FUEL TANK COMPARTMENT OF BOATS CONSTRUCTED OR DECKED OVER AFTER APRIL 25, 1940, USING GASOLINE AS FUEL AND OTHER FUELS HAVING A FLASHPOINT OF 110°F OR LESS. THERE SHALL BE AT LEAST ONE EXHAUST DUCT INSTALLED SO AS TO EXTEND TO THE LOWER PORTION OF THE BILGE AND AT LEAST ONE INTAKE DUCT INSTALLED SO AS

TO EXTEND TO A POINT MIDWAY TO THE BILGE OR AT LEAST BELOW THE LEVEL OF THE CARBURETOR AIR INTAKE.

BELL, WHISTLE- NONE.

PFD (PERSONAL FLOTATION DEVICES)- ONE TYPE I, II, III OR IV ON BOARD.

FIRE EXTINGUISHER/PORTABLE- WHEN NO FIXED FIRE EXTINGUISHING SYSTEM IS INSTALLED IN MACHINERY SPACE(S):

AT LEAST B-I TYPE APPROVED HAND PORTABLE FIRE EXTINGUISHER. (NOT REQUIRED ON OUTBOARD MOTORBOATS LESS THAN 26 FEET IN LENGTH IF THE CONSTRUCTION OF SUCH MOTORBOATS WILL NOT PERMIT THE ENTRAPMENT OF EXPLOSIVE OR FLAMMABLE GASES OR VAPORS.)

WHEN A FIXED FIRE EXTINGUISHING SYSTEM IS INSTALLED IN MACHINERY SPACE(S), ONE LESS B-I TYPE EXTINGUISHER IS REQUIRED.

2. 16 FEET TO LESS THAN 26 FEET IN LENGTH:

BACK-FIRE FLAME ARRESTER- SAME AS FOR SECTION 1.

VENTILATION- SAME AS FOR SECTION 1.

BELL- NONE.

WHISTLE- ONE HAND, MOUTH OR POWER-OPERATED WHISTLE, AUDIBLE AT LEAST ONE-HALF MILE.

PFD (PERSONAL FLOTATION DEVICES)- ONE TYPE I, II OR III FOR EACH PERSON PLUS ONE THROWABLE TYPE IV ON BOARD.

FIRE EXTINGUISHER/PORTABLE- SAME AS FOR SECTION 1.

3. 26 FEET TO LESS THAN 40 FEET IN LENGTH:

BACK-FIRE FLAME ARRESTER- SAME AS FOR SECTION 1.

VENTILATION- SAME AS FOR SECTION 1.

BELL- ONE, WHICH WHEN STRUCK, PRODUCES A CLEAR, BELL-LIKE TONE.

WHISTLE- ONE HAND OR POWER-OPERATED, AUDIBLE AT LEAST 1 MILE.

PFD (Personal Flotation Devices)- same as for Section 2.

Fire Extinguisher/Portable- at least two B-I type approved portable fire extinguishers; or at least one B-II type approved portable fire extinguisher. When an approved fixed system is installed, one less B-I type is required.

4. 40 feet to not more than 65 feet in length:

Back-Fire Flame Arrester- same as for Section 1.

Ventilation- same as for Section 1.

Bell- same as for Section 3.

Whistle- one power-operated, audible at least 1 mile.

PFD (Personal Flotation Devices)- same as for Section 2.

Fire Extinguisher/Portable- at least three B-I type approved fire extinguishers; or at least one B-I type plus one B-II type approved portable fire extinguisher. When an approved fixed system is installed, one less B-I type is required.

Note: Fire extinguishing equipment requirement for motor vessels greater than 65 feet in length can be found in Title 46, Code of Federal Regulations, Part 25 and in the U.S. Coast Guard publication "Rules and Regulations for Uninspected Vessels, Sub-chapter C" (CG-258).

Notice the mention of *Personal Flotation Devices.* Coast Guard attention to such lifesaving gear has developed a classification into five separate types. And the classifications differ, not only by size and shape; they also involve the effectiveness of the device to keep a person safely afloat. The Coast Guard describes them in these terms:

Type I PFD is any approved wearable device designed to turn an unconscious person in the water from a face-downward position to a vertical or slightly backward position, and to have more than 20 pounds of buoyancy. Recommended for offshore cruising.

This appliance is, in essence, a **life preserver.**

TYPE II PFD IS ANY APPROVED WEARABLE DEVICE DESIGNED TO TURN AN UNCONSCIOUS PERSON FROM A FACE-DOWN POSITION TO A FACE-UP VERTICAL OR SLIGHTLY BACKWARD POSITION AND TO HAVE AT LEAST 15.5 POUNDS OF BUOYANCY. RECOMMENDED FOR CLOSER INSHORE CRUISING.

This one, more wearable than a life preserver, is a **buoyant vest.**

TYPE III PFD IS ANY APPROVED WEARABLE DEVICE DESIGNED TO KEEP A CONSCIOUS PERSON IN A VERTICAL OR SLIGHTLY BACKWARD POSITION AND TO HAVE AT LEAST 15.5 POUNDS OF BUOYANCY. WHILE TYPE III HAS THE SAME BUOYANCY AS A TYPE II PFD, IT HAS A LESS TURNING MOMENT. IT DOES, HOWEVER, ALLOW A GREATER WEARING COMFORT AND IS PARTICULARLY USEFUL WHEN WATER SKIING, SAILING, HUNTING OR ENGAGED IN OTHER SUCH WATER SPORTS. IT IS RECOMMENDED FOR USE ON LAKES, IMPOUNDMENTS AND CLOSE INSHORE OPERATION.

This one has been described as a **special purpose water safety buoyant** device...the water-skiier's bandolier of buoyancy.

TYPE IV PFD IS ANY APPROVED DEVICE DESIGNED TO BE THROWN TO A PERSON IN THE WATER AND NOT BE WORN. IT IS DESIGNED TO HAVE AT LEAST 16.5 POUNDS OF BUOYANCY.

An example is the **buoyant cushion** or **ring life buoy.**

TYPE V PFD IS ANY APPROVED WEARABLE DEVICE DESIGNED FOR A SPECIFIC AND RESTRICTED USE...THE ONLY PRESENTLY APPROVED DEVICE THAT FALLS INTO THE TYPE V DESIGNATION IS THE "WORK VEST"...FOR USE BY PERSONS WORKING AROUND MERCHANT VESSELS.

No mention is made of Type V as required equipment on pleasure boats.

The aim is to use these designations in specifying what type must be aboard what class and length of boat. A rowboat, for example, could get by with only one PFD aboard, and of any type from I through IV. But a 50-foot cruiser would need a I, II or III for each person and also one throwable Type IV in an accessible onboard position.

Note also the mention in the Equipment Section of fire extinguishers as B-I and B-II. This refers to a Coast Guard classification by size and type of fire involved. Fires come in three kinds: **Class A** is a fire of ordinary combustible materials; **Class B** is a petroleum fire...gasoline, oil, grease, etc.; **Class C** is an electrical fire. The letter in an extinguisher designation refers to the class of fire on which the device is considered most effective. And movable extinguishers come in five **sizes. I** is the smallest. It includes a 1½-gallon foam, a 4-pound CO_2 pressure type, a 2-pound dry chemical, and a 2½-pound Freon. **II** describes a 2½-gallon foam, a 15-pound CO_2 pressure and a 10-pound dry chemical. These two sizes are rated as **hand-portable.** The remaining three sizes refer to **semi-portable** extinguishers requiring side boys or a hand truck to be moved about; and they would seldom be found aboard a pleasure boat. **III** is a 12-gallon foam, 35-pound CO_2 or 20-pound dry chemical. **IV** is a 20-gallon foam, 50-pound CO_2 or 30-pound dry chemical. And **V** is a 40-gallon foam, 100-pound CO_2 or 50-pound dry chemical. Unlikely would it be for someone to snatch such a heavy container off the bulkhead and skip down the deck, spraying embers as he went. So the Equipment Schedule limits its scope to the first two sizes. And when it indicates B-I as a required type, it specifies one of the smallest size and suitable for petroleum fires. Commonly used to fit the bill is a 2-pound dry chemical type. And B-II requires a larger extinguisher for gasoline, oil or grease fires. . .a 10-pound dry chemical, for example.

Other operating rules presently set out for pleasure vessels by the Coast Guard are these:

NUMBERING:

> THE FEDERAL BOAT SAFETY ACT OF 1971 AND ITS IMPLEMENTING REGULATIONS ESTABLISHED A STANDARD SYSTEM FOR THE NUMBERING OF UNDOCUMENTED VESSELS. UNDOCUMENTED VESSELS ARE TO BE NUMBERED (REGISTERED) IN THE STATE IN WHICH THE VESSEL IS PRINCIPALLY USED. IF A VESSEL IS EQUIPPED WITH PROPULSION MACHINERY OF ANY TYPE, AND IS USED PRINCIPALLY ON THE WATERS SUBJECT TO THE JURISDICTION OF THE UNITED STATES IN NEW HAMPSHIRE, WASHINGTON, ALASKA, OR THE DISTRICT OF COLUMBIA, THE CERTIFICATE OF NUMBER WILL BE ISSUED BY THE U.S. COAST GUARD. A VESSEL USED PRINCIPALLY ON THE HIGH SEAS IS REQUIRED TO BE NUMBERED BY THE STATE IN WHICH IT IS PRINCIPALLY USED WHEN NOT ON THE HIGH SEAS.
>
> CERTIFICATE OF NUMBER
>
> THE NUMBER ISSUED TO A VESSEL IS SHOWN ON THE CERTIFICATE OF NUMBER. THE CERTIFICATE OF NUMBER MUST BE ON BOARD WHENEVER THE VESSEL IS IN USE. A NUMBER AWARDED BY THE U.S. COAST GUARD IS VALID FOR 3 YEARS.
>
> VALIDATION STICKER
>
> WITH EACH CERTIFICATE OF NUMBER ISSUED BY THE U.S. COAST GUARD, TWO COLOR-CODED VALIDATION STICKERS ARE ISSUED TO SHOW THAT THE VESSEL IS VALIDLY NUMBERED. THE VALIDATION STICKERS MUST BE DISPLAYED WITHIN 6 INCHES OF THE NUMBER.

Display of Number and Validation Stickers

The vessel's number must be painted on or permanently attached to each side of the forward half of the vessel (the bow), and no other number may be displayed thereon. Numbers are to read left to right, be in plain vertical block characters, be of a color contrasting with the background, be distinctly visible and legible, and be not less than 3 inches in height. Example: OK 2334 FG or OK-2334-FG.

Numbering Systems

A number issued may be valid for not more than 3 years. A State numbering system may require the numbering of any vessel subject to the jurisdiction of the State unless prohibited by Federal regulation. Each State with an approved numbering system must recognize the validity of a number issued by the U.S. Coast Guard or by another State having an approved system for a period of at least 60 days before requiring numbering in the new State of Principal use.

Information about numbering systems is available from State agencies, U.S. Coast Guard units, and marine dealers.

Notification of Changes Required

When a *vessel* is lost, destroyed, abandoned, stolen, recovered, or transferred, the person whose name appears on the certificate of number as the owner shall within 15 days notify the authority which numbered the vessel.

If the Certificate of Number is lost or destroyed or the owner changes his address, he shall notify the issuing authority within 15 days.

A person whose name appears as the owner of a vessel on a Certificate of Number shall surrender the certificate in the manner prescribed by the issuing authority within 15 days after it becomes invalid for any reason.

Accident Reports:

When as a result of an occurrence that involves a vessel or its equipment, a person dies or disappears from a vessel, the operator shall, without delay, notify the nearest U.S. Coast Guard or State boating authority of:

a. The date, time, and exact location of the occurrence.

b. The name of each person who died or disappeared.

c. The number and name of the vessel.

d. The names and addresses of the owner and operator.

(If the operator cannot give this notice, each person on board shall notify that authority, *or determine that such notice has been given.*

The operator of a vessel shall submit the Boating Accident Report Form (CG-3865) or proper State form within 48 hours of an accident in which:

a. A person dies within 24 hours.

b. A person loses consciousness or receives medical treatment or is disabled for more than 24 hours.

c. A person disappears from the vessel under circumstances that indicate death or injury.

Accidents must be reported within 5 days if damage to the vessel and other property totals more than $100 or an earlier report is not required.

Enforcement and Penalties:

U.S. Coast Guard vessels are identified by a distinctive stripe, the words *Coast Guard* on the side of the vessel, the Coast Guard Ensign, and are manned by uniformed personnel. Coast Guard law enforcement personnel may also be found aboard other vessels displaying the Coast Guard Ensign.

A vessel underway, upon being hailed by a Coast Guard vessel or patrol boat, is required to stop immediately and lay to, or maneuver in such a way as to permit the boarding officer to come aboard. Failure to stop to permit boarding may subject the operator or owner to a maximum penalty of $500.

A civil penalty of $500 may be imposed by the Coast Guard for failure to comply with numbering requirements, to observe the Rules of the Road, to comply with equipment requirements, to report a boating accident, etc.

NEGLIGENT OR GROSSLY NEGLIGENT OPERATION of a vessel which endangers life, limb, or property is prohibited by law. A civil penalty may be imposed by the Coast Guard for negligent operation, or the operator may be subjected to a fine up to $1,000, or imprisonment of not more than 1 year, or both, for the criminal offense of GROSSLY NEGLIGENT OPERATION.

Some examples of actions that may constitute negligent or grossly negligent operation under certain circumstances are:

A. Operating recklessly in swimming areas,
B. Overloading.
C. Operating while under the influence of alcohol or drugs and recognizable by erratic operation,
D. Excessive speed in the vicinity of other boats, or in dangerous waters,
E. Unsafe water skiing practices,
F. Operating in clearly dangerous areas,
G. Operating without proper lights at night,
H. Bow, seatback, gunwale, or transom riding.

If a Coast Guard boarding officer observes a specifically defined unsafe condition and determines that an ESPECIALLY HAZARDOUS CONDITION exists, he may direct the operator to take immediate steps to correct the condition, including returning to mooring. The specific unsafe conditions for which the boatman may presently be terminated, are:

A. Insufficient lifesaving devices (PFD),
B. Insufficient firefighting devices,
C. Overloaded condition,
D. Improper navigation light display,
E. Fuel leakage,
F. Fuel in the bilges,
G. Improper ventilation,
H. Improper backfire flame control.

IF THE OPERATOR REFUSES TO COMPLY WITH THE ORDER TO TERMINATE UNSAFE USE OF THE BOAT, HE CAN BE CITED FOR FAILURE TO COMPLY WITH THE DIRECTIONS OF A COAST GUARD BOARDING OFFICER (33 CFR 177.05) AS WELL AS FOR THE SPECIFIC STATUTORY OR REGULATORY VIOLATIONS OR PROVISIONS WHICH WERE THE BASIS FOR THE TERMINATION ORDER.

Water Pollution:

The Refuse Act of 1899 prohibits the throwing, discharging, or depositing of any refuse matter of any kind (including trash, garbage, oil, and other liquid pollutants) into the waters of the United States to a distance of three miles from the coastline. The

Federal Water Pollution Control Act prohibits the discharge of oil or hazardous substances into the waters of the United States to twelve miles offshore. You must immediately notify the U.S. Coast Guard if your vessel or facility discharges oil or hazardous substances into the water. Those who fail to protect the environment by not obeying these provisions may be subject to severe civil and criminal penalties.

You must also help to ensure that others obey the law. You are encouraged to report polluting discharges which you observe to the nearest U.S. Coast Guard office. Report the following information:

A. Location,
B. Source,
C. Size,
D. Color,
E. Substance,
F. Time observed.

Do not attempt to take samples of any chemical discharge. If uncertain as to the identity of any discharge, avoid flame, physical contact, or inhalation of fumes.

Vessel Examination:

To determine if your motorboat meets Federal requirements as well as further recommended safety standards, contact a member of the Coast Guard Auxiliary for a free Courtesy Motorboat Examination. A decal is awarded to motorboats which pass the examination. If your boat does not have the proper equipment NO *report is made to any law enforcement authority.* The Auxiliary examiner will advise you of the deficiencies so that you can correct them. If your motorboat is less than 16 feet you can request a *Federal Equipment Check* from the Auxiliary or from a Coast Guard Boating Safety Detachment (BOSDET). This check is limited to Federal equipment requirements and a distinctive decal is awarded to motorboats which pass.

There is really little point in further itemization in this vein. A round of visits to government offices will produce enough official schedules and pamphlets to fill a seabag. In that seabag, though, should be a copy of CG-290. . . the latest edition. This pamphlet, entitled **Federal Requirements for Recreational Boats,** condenses such material as we have discussed on equipment, reports, operation and the like. A visit to the Boating Safety Branch of Coast Guard District Headquarters is well worth the time. You'll come away, not only with CG-290, but with the definite impression that the Coast Guard's business is your safe pleasure. Education has been said to be, not knowing the answer, but rather where to find it. The alert boatowner should make as part of his routine to learn from official sources the current answers to old and new questions as they should appear.

DOCUMENTS

DOCUMENTS	PAGE
Bill of Sale of Enrolled or Licensed Yacht	85
Consolidated Certificate of Enrollment and Yacht License	86
Preferred Ship Mortgage	87
Satisfaction of Mortgage	88
Oaths on Registry, License, or Enrollment and License of Vessel	90
Master's Oath on Registry, License, or Enrollment and License	91
Application for Simplified Method of Admeasurement	92
Vessel Documentation Work Sheet	94
Master Carpenter's Certificate	95
Designation of Home Port of Vessel	96
Application of Owner For and Notice of Award of Official Number and Signal Letters	97 & 98

DEPARTMENT OF TRANSPORTATION
U.S. Coast Guard
CG-1346 (Rev. 8-67)

Form Approved.
Budget Bureau No. 04-R3043.

The United States of America

DEPARTMENT OF TRANSPORTATION
U.S. COAST GUARD

BILL OF SALE OF ENROLLED OR LICENSED YACHT

To all to whom these Presents shall come, Greeting:

Know Ye, That[1] .... (Name of seller) .... (Interest owned)

....

....

....

....

....

(hereinafter called the seller(s)) of the .... (Rig) .... vessel called the .... of .... net tons, or thereabouts, for and in consideration of the sum of .... dollars, lawful money of the United States of America, to .... in hand paid, before the sealing and delivery of these presents, the receipt whereof .... do hereby acknowledge and .... therewith fully satisfied, contented, and paid, ha bargained and sold, and by these presents do bargain and sell the interest in the herein described vessel more fully set forth below unto the said[2] .... (Name of buyer) .... (Interest transferred)

....

....

....

....

....

....

(hereinafter called the buyer(s)) .... executors, administrators, successors, and assigns, together with an equal interest in the masts, bowsprit, sails, boats, anchors, cables, tackle, furniture, and all other necessaries thereunto appertaining and belonging; the[3] CERTIFICATE OF ENROLLMENT AND YACHT LICENSE of which said vessel is as follows, viz.:

[1] Here insert the name and address of each seller and the part owned by him (as "sole," "one-half," etc.).
[2] Here insert the name and address of each buyer and the part conveyed to him (as "sole," "one-half," etc.).
[3] Strike out the words "Certificate of Enrollment and" when yacht is not enrolled.

A TRUE COPY OF THE LATEST CONSOLIDATED CERTIFICATE OF ENROLLMENT AND YACHT LICENSE

PERMANENT OR TEMPORARY	The United States of America	OFFICIAL NO.	CONDENSED RADIO CALL AND SIGNAL LETTERS
.... Certificate No.	____________[1] ____________[2]		

Measured at ...., *19*......

Rebuilt at ...., *19*......

Remeasured at ...., *19*...... *Horsepower* ....

CONSOLIDATED CERTIFICATE OF ENROLLMENT AND YACHT LICENSE†

LICENSE OF YACHT UNDER TWENTY TONS‡

In conformity to Title L, "Regulation of Vessels in Domestic Commerce," and Chapter Two, Title XLVII, "Regulation of Commerce and Navigation," of the Revised Statutes of the United States, and to "An act to amend Sections 4214 and 4218 of the Revised Statutes Relating to Yachts," approved August 20, 1912

....

having taken and subscribed the oath .... required by law, and having sworn .... that

....

....

....

....

....

.... citizen.. of the United States and the sole owner.... of the vessel called the ....

...., of ....

and that the said vessel was built in the year 1......., at .... of ....

as appears by ....

and .... having certified that

the said vessel is a ....; that she has

.... deck.., ... mast .., a .... stem, and a .... stern; that her

register length is .... 10 feet, her register breadth .... 10 feet, her register depth .... 10 feet,

her height .... 10 feet; that she measures as follows:

	TONS	100ths
Capacity under tonnage deck		
Capacity between decks above tonnage deck		
Capacity of enclosures on the upper deck, viz: Forecastle......; bridge......; poop......; break......; houses—deck ...., side ...., mast ...., trunks .....; excess hatchways.....; light and air ......;		
GROSS TONNAGE		
Deductions under Section 4153, Revised Statutes, as amended (Sec. 77, title 46, U.S. Code):		
Crew space, ...; master's cabin, ...;		
Steering gear, ...; anchor gear, ...; boatswain's stores ....;		
Chart house, ...; donkeys engine and boiler, ...; radiohouse, ...;		
Storage of sails, ...; propelling power (actual space ....), ...;		
TOTAL DEDUCTIONS		
NET TONNAGE		

The following-described spaces, and no others, have been omitted, viz: Forepeak ...., afterpeak ...., other spaces (except double bottoms) for water ballast ....; open forecastle ...., open bridge ...., open poop........, open shelter deck ...., open houses ...., cabins ...., companions ...., galley ...., skylights ...., wheelhouse ...., water closets ....; anchor gear ...., donkey engine and boiler ...., steering gear ...., light and air spaces ...., other machinery spaces ...., ...

§and .... having agreed to the description and measurement above specified, the said vessel has been duly ENROLLED at this PORT;

And ...., the master, having sworn that he is a citizen of the United States, that this vessel, used and employed exclusively as a PLEASURE VESSEL or designed as a model of naval architecture, shall not, while this license continues in force, transport merchandise or carry passengers for pay, or engage in any unlawful trade, nor in any way violate the revenue laws of the United States, and shall comply with the laws in all other respects:

LICENSE is hereby granted for the said YACHT to proceed from port to port in the United States without entering or clearing at the customhouse, and to foreign ports without clearing in the United States. This LICENSE will continue and be in force for ONE YEAR from the date hereof, and no longer.

Given under my hand and seal at the Port of ....

District of ...., this .... day of ....

in the year one thousand nine hundred and ....

....

____________________________[4]

†Strike out line, if vessel is licensed only. ‡Strike out line, if vessel is enrolled. §Strike out this and following line, if vessel is licensed only.
[1] Insert "Treasury Department" or "Department of Transportation" as appropriate.
[2] Insert "Bureau of Customs" or "U.S. Coast Guard" as appropriate.
[4] Insert "Collector of Customs" or "Documentation Officer" as appropriate.

Preferred · Ship Mortgage

THIS MORTGAGE, made this..........day of ...., 19...., between ....hereinafter called the Mortgagor, and ....hereinafter called the Mortgagee:

WITNESSETH:

WHEREAS, the Mortgagor is the sole owner of the hereinafter described vessel.

WHEREAS, the Mortgagor is justly indebted to the Mortgagee in the sum of .... Dollars, ($..................) and to secure the payment of said thereof with charges has executed and delivered this preferred mortgage and note to the Mortgagee;

NOW, THEREFORE, THIS MORTGAGE WITNESSETH:

That in consideration of the premises and of the sum of One Dollar ($1.00) to the mortgagor duly paid by the Mortgagee, receipt whereof is hereby acknowledged, and in order to secure the payment of the said principal sum of ....Dollars, ($....................) and charges precomputed at the rate of $............. per $100 per year on the original principal amount and the payment of any advancements that shall hereafter be made, and of the said note and the performance of all the covenants and conditions herein, the Mortgagor has granted, bargained, sold, conveyed, transferred, assigned, remised, released, mortgaged, set over, and confirmed and by these presents does grant, bargain, sell, conv.·y, transfer, assign, remise, release, mortgage, set over, and confirm unto the Mortgagee, his heirs, administrators, executors, successors and assignees all of the following:

The certain........................(rig)........................vessel called .... of..............(home port).............. official number.......................of................. gross tons.

The maturity date of this mortage is:..................................

DEPARTMENT OF
TRANSPORTATION
U. S. COAST GUARD
CG-1363 (Rev. 11-67)

SATISFACTION OF MORTGAGE

Form Approved Bureau of Budget
No. 004-R3046

DEPARTMENT OF TRANSPORTATION
U. S. COAST GUARD

STATE OF ____________ }
COUNTY OF ____________ } ss:

DO HEREBY CERTIFY That a certain INDENTURE OF MORTGAGE, bearing date the day of , one thousand nine hundred and made and executed by

to secure the payment of Dollars, on of the or vessel called the , official number , net tonnage , and recorded in the office of the Documentation Officer at in Preferred* Mortgage Book No. , Instrument No. , on the day of , in the year 1 , at o'clock minutes in the noon, is paid, and do consent that the same be discharged of record.

Dated the day of , 19

In presence of [SEAL.]

STATE OF†
COUNTY OF } ss:

Be it known, That on this day of , 19 , personally appeared before me,‡

and acknowledged the within instrument to be free act and deed.

In testimony whereof, I have hereunto set my hand and seal this day of , A. D. 19

[SEAL]

Received for record , 19 , h. m. m., and recorded in Preferred* Mortgage Book No. , Instrument No.

Recording Clerk.

*Strike out the word "Preferred" if inappropriate.
†This acknowledgment may be made to conform to requirements of State laws.
‡If the mortgagee is a corporation, write:

________________________, "who being duly sworn, deposed and said that he is the president, secretary, or other officer or agent [the acknowledgment of an instrument by a corporation must be made by some officer thereof authorized to execute it by the board of directors of the corporation. If the corporation has no seal, that fact must be stated in place of the statement respecting the seal], of the [name of corporation], the corporation which is described in and executed the within instrument, and that he knows the seal of the said corporation, and that it is affixed and was so affixed to the within instrument by order of the board of directors of the said corporation at whose order he signed his name and acknowledged the within instrument to be the free act and deed of the said corporation," or such other words as may be required by State laws.

GPO 958-942

DEPARTMENT OF TRANSPORTATION
U. S. COAST GUARD
CG-1259 (Rev. 6-69)

Form approved.
Budget Bureau No. 04-R3037

OATHS ON REGISTRY, LICENSE, OR ENROLLMENT AND LICENSE OF VESSEL

HOWARD HARTRY, INC.
P. O. BOX 351
SAN PEDRO, CALIFORNIA 9073

OATH OF OFFICER OR AGENT OF INCORPORATED COMPANY

PORT	SERVICE	HORSEPOWER
NAME OF OFFICER OR AGENT	TITLE [1]	ADDRESS OF OFFICER OF THE CORPORATION
FULL CORPORATE NAME OF CORPORATION AND INTERNAL REVENUE SERVICE EMPLOYER NO. [2]		
STATE IN WHICH INCORPORATED	BUSINESS ADDRESS OF CORPORATION *(Include Zip Code)*	RIG
NAME OF VESSEL		HOME PORT OF VESSEL

OFFICIAL NO	GROSS TONNAGE	NET TONNAGE	YEAR BUILT	PLACE OF BUILD

3

MATERIAL	AS APPEARS BY (DOCUMENT)	NO	PORT WHERE ISSUED	DATE ISSUED

CAUSE OF SURRENDER

PASSENGERS TO BE CARRIED ☐ Six or less ☐ More than six ☐ None

FREIGHT TO BE CARRIED ☐ Owner's property ☐ For hire ☐ None

NAME OF PRESENT MASTER	CITY IN OR NEAR WHICH PRESENT MASTER WAS BORN	STATE OR COUNTRY	DATE OF BIRTH

COMPLETE THIS SECTION ONLY IF PRESENT MASTER IS A NATURALIZED CITIZEN

NAME OF COURT BEFORE WHICH PRESENT MASTER WAS NATURALIZED

DISTRICT, COUNTY, OR STATE	DATE OF NATURALIZATION	NATURALIZATION CERTIFICATE NO

This vessel ☐ is ☐ is not within the customs district where the vessel document is to be issued.

PRESENT LOCATION OF VESSEL [4]

I swear that the information given above is true and correct to the best of my knowledge and belief;

that the corporation named above is the sole owner of the vessel identified herein;

that the president or other chief executive officer and the chairman of the board of directors of said corporation are citizens of the United States and no more of its directors than a minority of the number necessary to constitute a quorum are noncitizens;

[5] that 75 per centum of the interest in said corporation is owned by citizens of the United States; that the title to 75 per centum of the stock of said corporation is vested in citizens of the United States free from any trust or fiduciary obligation in favor of any person not a citizen of the United States and that such proportion of the voting power of said corporation is vested in citizens of the United States;

that through no contract or understanding is it so arranged that more than 25 per centum of the voting power of said corporation may be exercised, directly or indirectly, in behalf of any person who is not a citizen of the United States;

that by no means whatsoever is the control of any interest in said corporation in excess of 25 per centum conferred upon or permitted to be exercised by any person who is not a citizen of the United States;

[6] that no subject or citizen of any foreign prince or state is, directly or indirectly, by way of trust, confidence, or otherwise, interested therein, or in the profits or issues thereof;

[7] that the present master is a citizen of the United States.

[8] I also swear that all equipments or any part thereof, including boats, purchased for, or the repair parts or materials to be used, or the expenses of repairs made in any foreign country upon said vessel within the year immediately preceding the date of this application, have been duly reported and accounted for under the provisions of sections 257 and 258, title 19, and section 272, title 46, United States Code, and the duties thereon have been duly paid.

SIGNATURE [9]

SUBSCRIBED AND SWORN TO BEFORE ME			SIGNATURE OF NOTARY PUBLIC OR DOCUMENTATION OFFICER
DAY	MONTH	YEAR	

1 Insert "President," "Secretary," "Specially authorized officer," or "Agent" as the case may be.

2 If vessel is owned by more than one owner, only the number of the managing owner, if one has been designated, or one of the owners, shall be shown.

3 See section 3.2, Customs Regulations, for means whereby vessel may become entitled to American registry. If the vessel falls within classes 4, 5, 6, or 7 of that section, the appropriate clause required by section 3.18, Customs Regulations, shall be inserted here.

4 If vessel is not within the customs district where the vessel document is to be issued.

5 Strike out this section if vessel is not to engage in coastwise trade.

6 Strike out this section in case of licensed vessel of less than 20 tons.

7 Strike out this section in case of registered vessel, if the master is within the district where registry is to be made, and in the case of licensed or enrolled and licensed vessel.

8 Strike out this section in case of registered vessel.

9 The officer or agent of the corporation subscribing to this oath, if other than the president or secretary, shall present a written instrument attested by the corporate seal, authorizing him to act in this behalf.

PREVIOUS EDITION IS OBSOLETE

SEE REVERSE

MASTER'S OATH ON REGISTRY, LICENSE, OR ENROLLMENT AND LICENSE

(Section 4144, and section 4320 R.S., as amended; 46 U.S.C. 22 and 262)

THIS OATH MUST NOT BE USED FOR RENEWALS OF LICENSES BY ENDORSEMENTS

NAME OF MASTER			ADDRESS
RIG	NAME OF VESSEL	OFFICIAL NO.	
CITY (OR NEAREST CITY) OF BIRTH	STATE OR COUNTRY OF BIRTH		DATE OF BIRTH

COMPLETE THIS SECTION ONLY IF YOU ARE A NATURALIZED CITIZEN

NAME OF COURT BEFORE WHICH YOU WERE NATURALIZED		
DISTRICT, COUNTY, OR STATE	DATE OF NATURALIZATION	NATURALIZATION CERTIFICATE NO

EMPLOYMENT OF VESSEL[1]

I swear that the information given above is true and correct to the best of my knowledge and belief; that I am a citizen of the United States;

[2] that the license granted to the vessel identified herein shall not be used for any other vessel or for any other employment than that specified above or in any trade or business whereby the revenue of the United States may be defrauded.

SIGNATURE OF MASTER

SUBSCRIBED AND SWORN TO BEFORE ME:			SIGNATURE OF NOTARY PUBLIC OR DOCUMENTATION OFFICER
DAY	MONTH	YEAR	

[1] Insert "coasting trade and mackerel fishery," "whale fishery," "mackerel fishery," "cod fishery," "pleasure," (in case of a yacht), or "coasting and foreign trade" (in case of enrolled and licensed for foreign and coasting trade on the northern, northeastern, and northwestern frontiers, otherwise than by sea).

[2] Strike out this section in case of registered vessel.

Department of Transportation

UNITED STATES COAST GUARD

Date: ____________________

Officer in Charge, Marine Inspection (LA-LB)
2035 Customhouse
300 South Ferry Street
Terminal Island, California 90731

Dear Sir:

Application is hereby submitted for the simplified method of admeasurement for the following vessel intended solely for use as a pleasure craft (yacht) as provided for in Sections 2.101 thru 2.103, C.G. Regulations.

NAME OF VESSEL ____________________ Rig ____________________
(Gas Screw/Oil Screw/Other (specify)

NAME OF BUILDER ____________________ BUILT OF ____________________
(Wood/steel/fiberglass/etc.)

PLACE OF BUILD ____________________ YEAR COMPLETED __________
(City) (State or Country)

BUILDER'S HULL, MODEL OR SERIAL NUMBER ____________________

REGISTRATION NUMBER ____________________
(State, U.S. Coast Guard or Previous Documentation No.)

LOCATION OF ENGINE ____________________
(Indicate Inboard or Outboard type)

VESSEL PRESENTLY BERTHED AT ____________________ DATE LAUNCHED: ________

OVERALL DIMENSIONS: Length ____________ Breadth ____________ Depth ________
(as defined in instructions on reverse side)

THE VESSEL (is) (is not) designed for sailing
(as defined in instructions on reverse side)

Address of Owner ____________________

____________________ ____________________
(Business and/or Home Phone Number) (Social Security or Internal Revenue No.)

____
(Signature of Owner)

DEFINITION OF TERMS

(a) "Over-all length" means the horizontal distance between the foremost part of the stem and the aftermost part of the stern, excluding bow-sprits, bumpkins, rudders, outboard motor brackers, and similar fittings or attachments. (see figure A)

(b) "Overall-breadth" is the horizontal distance, excluding rub rails, from the outside of the skin (outside planking or plating) on one side to the outside of the skin on the other, taken at the widest part of the hull. (see figure B)

(c) "Overall depth" is the vertical distance taken at or near midships from a line drawn horizontally through the uppermost edges of the skin at the sides of the hull (excluding the cap rail and trunks, cabins or deckhouses) to the outboard face of the bottom skin of the hull. This excludes the keel unless the keel is covered by the skin. (see figure C)

(d) "Vessel designed for sailing" means a vessel, whether or not equipped with an auxiliary motor, which has the fine lines of a sailing craft and is in fact propelled by sail or capable of being propelled by sail, other than a mere steadying sail.

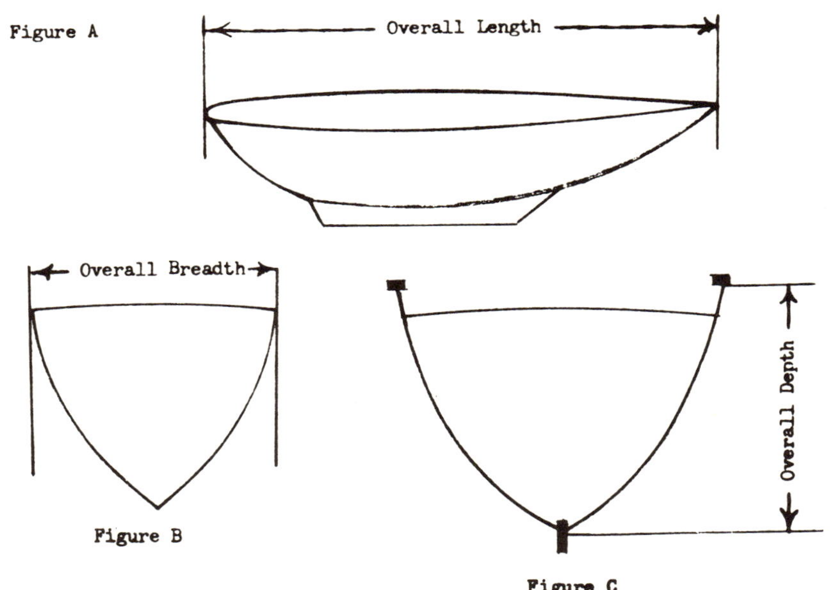

UNDOCUMENTED VESSEL DATE:____________________

VESSEL DOCUMENTATION WORK SHEET

(date items when received or completed; strike out those not applicable)

__________SCREW______________________________________ HOME PORT:____________________

O?N:______________ GROSS:__________ NET:____________ HAILING PORT:____________________

EX NAMES AND NUMBERS:____

__________ 1. Admeasurement Arranged For FEE:____________________

__________ 2. Bill(s) of Sale (CG 1342/1344/1346) FEE:____________________

__________ 3. State History of Vessel FEE:____________________

__________ 4. Abstract of Title under Old Style C.G. Motor Boat Number

__________ 5. Certificate of State Ownership (Pink Slip)

__________ 6. Master Carpenter's Certificate

__________ 7. Application for award of official number

__________ 8. Designation of Home Port (CG 1319)

__________ 9. Managing Owner Letter

__________ 10. Affadivit of Citizenship (MA 4557/4558/4559/IC 27-227)

__________ 11. Oaths on Application(CG 1258/1259)

__________ 12. Certified Copy of Articles of Incorporation or Certificate of Good Standing

__________ 13. Certificate as to Organization of Corporation

__________ 14. Certificate of Fictitious Name (DBA)

__________ 15. Power of Attorney

__________ 16. Certificate of Ownership (when requested to obtain from U.S.C.G.)FEE:__________

__________ 17. Marking Certificate

__________ 18.

__________ 19.

__________ 20.

__________ 21. Paperwork forwarded to U.S.C.G. Documentation Office at ____________________

__________ 22. Document returned

FOREIGN BUILD:

__________ 1. Master Carpenter's Certificate or Letter of Consent

__________ 2. Evidence of Duty Paid

__________ 3. Certificate of Bona Fide

__________ 4. Sea worthy Certificate

__________ 5. Copy of foreign registry

__________ 6.

__________ 7.

PREFERRED SHIP MORTGAGE:

__________ 1. Notes received from mortgagee

__________ 2. Citizenship Affadivit of Mortgagee received

__________ 3. Vessel Document received

__________ 4. P.S.M. prepared, signed and notarized FEE:____________________

__________ 5. P.S.M. filed with U.S.C.G.

__________ 6. Recorded P.S.M. returned

REMARKS: 1. Seller:____

2. Buyer:____

3. Mortgagee:____

4. Yacht Broker:____

INVOICE: NO.____________________ DATED____________________ FORWARD TO OWNER WITH VESSEL DOCUMENT AND CERTIFIED COPIES OF P.S.M. ON CERTIFIED MAIL #____________________

ORIGINAL P.S.M. FORWARDED TO MORTGAGEE UNDER CERTIFIED MAIL #____________________

Reprinted by permission of Howard Hartry, Customhouse Broker, Los Angeles Harbor.

DEPARTMENT OF TRANSPORTATION
U. S. COAST GUARD
CG-1261 (Rev. 6-67)

Form Approved Bureau of Budget
No. 04-R3038

MASTER CARPENTER'S CERTIFICATE
(BUILDER'S CERTIFICATE)

PLACE	DATE	NAME OF MASTER OR PRINCIPAL CARPENTER

ADDRESS

RIG [1]

NAME OF THE VESSEL [2]	HULL NO.

VESSEL WAS BUILT (*Insert "By me," "Under my direction," or "By ....," giving firm or corporate name, if applicable*)

YEAR OF COMPLETION	PLACE WHERE BUILT [3]	MATERIAL OF BUILD [4]

NAME OF PERSON OR PERSONS FOR WHOM BUILT AND INDIVIDUAL INTEREST OWNED

NUMBER OF DECKS	NUMBER OF MASTS	CONTOUR OF STEM	SHAPE OF STERN

LENGTH OF VESSEL [5]	BREADTH OF VESSEL [5]	DEPTH OF VESSEL [5]
— /10 FEET	— /10 FEET	— /10 FEET

GROSS TONNAGE	NET TONNAGE

[1] Insert here the rig of the vessel. For a vessel having a steam engine write "steam side wheel," "steam stern wheel," "steam screw"; and for a vessel having an internal combustion engine write "gas (or oil) side wheel;" "gas (or oil) stern wheel," "gas (or oil) screw," or as the case may be.
[2] The name given herein shall be in exact agreement with the spelling as marked on the vessel itself.
[3] Write the name of the city or town at or nearest to which the vessel was built, and include the name of the state and country.
[4] Insert "wood," "iron," "steel," or as the case may be.
[5] Dimensions are to be calculated as specified in R.S. 4150.

THE FOLLOWING ADDITIONAL PARTICULARS SHALL BE GIVEN FOR THE ENGINE OF MACHINERY-PROPELLED VESSELS

TYPE OF ENGINE (*Reciprocating, beam, turbine, etc., if steam, oil, gas, etc., if internal combustion*)

PLACE WHERE BUILT	YEAR BUILT

BUILT BY

POWER (*Steam, heavy oil, light oil, gasoline, naphtha, etc.*)

NOTE.—An *oil* engine is an internal-combustion engine in which the fuel is injected into the air that is under compression in the cylinder; the combination is ignited by the heat generated from the compression (Diesel type), or from additional outside heat when that in the cylinder is not sufficient (Semi-Diesel type). A *gas* engine is also an internal combustion engine, but in it the fuel and air are admitted into the cylinder simultaneously and the combination is ignited by a spark.

I certify that the information given above is true and correct to the best of my knowledge and belief.

The master carpenter or builder shall not sign this certificate until he knows that the name as above written agrees *exactly* with that marked on the vessel.

SIGNATURE OF MASTER CARPENTER OR BUILDER

GPO 959-024

DEPARTMENT OF TRANSPORTATION
U. S. COAST GUARD
CG-1319 (Rev. 5-67)

Form approved.
Budget Bureau No. 48-R195.4

DESIGNATION OF HOME PORT OF VESSEL

DEPARTMENT OF TRANSPORTATION
UNITED STATES COAST GUARD

DATE ....

To: THE DOCUMENTATION OFFICER AT ....

In accordance with the provisions of the Act of February 16, 1925, I hereby designate ....

....

a port of documentation, as the home port of the ....
(Rig and name of vessel)

...., official number ....
and request your approval thereof. The vessel business of the owner or owners named below will be conducted at and from the following address: ....
(Street and Number, City, State and Zip Code)

Signature [1] .... Capacity [2] ....

Signature [1] .... Capacity [2] ....

Please type or print name above signature and indicate capacity in which applicant signs.

FORWARDED:

....
Documentation Officer.

Port:

Date:

Remarks:

APPROVAL:

The above designation is approved.

....
(Signature)

....
(Title)

....
(Port or place) (Date)

[1] In the case of corporate ownership, the application shall be signed in the corporate name by the president, secretary, or a specially authorized officer of the corporation or by an authorized agent. In the case of a firm or partnership, the firm or partnership name shall be signed either by a member of the firm or one of the partners, or by a duly authorized agent. In the case of individual ownership by two or more persons, one of the owners may sign his own name as "managing owner" provided there is filed with the collector a written authorization for him to act in that capacity signed by the owners of a majority interest in the vessel. The names of all the members of a firm or partnership owning a vessel and in the case of ownership by two or more individuals, the name and proportionate interest of each owner in a vessel shall be given.

[2] In every case, the capacity in which the person signs, whether as owner, managing owner, agent, member of firm, copartner, etc., shall be stated clearly after his signature in the space provided. If an individual executes the application in the name of a corporation, firm, or partnership, the capacity in which the organization name is signed, whether as owner, managing owner, authorized agent, etc., shall be shown immediately after the name of such organization and the capacity in which the individual signs as representative of the organization, whether as president, secretary, authorized agent, etc., shall be shown immediately following his signature.

This designation shall be filed in duplicate when filed with the Documentation Officer at the home port designated for the vessel; otherwise, in triplicate.

GPO 957-116

DEPARTMENT OF TRANSPORTATION
U. S. COAST GUARD
CG-1320 (Rev. 5-67)

Form Approved.
Budget Bureau No. 48-R196.6.

APPLICATION OF OWNER FOR AND NOTICE OF AWARD OF OFFICIAL NUMBER AND SIGNAL LETTERS

(To be filed in TRIPLICATE if presented to the Documentation Officer at the home port designated; in QUADRUPLICATE if presented at any other port.)

DEPARTMENT OF TRANSPORTATION
UNITED STATES COAST GUARD

Place ....
(Date)

): THE DOCUMENTATION OFFICER AT ....

Application is hereby made for an OFFICIAL NUMBER for the following-described vessel, which is ready for a arine document:

ame [1] .... Rig [2] ....
ervice [3] .... Horsepower [4] ....
ength .... Tonnages: Gross .... Net .... Builder's Hull No. ....
uilder [5] .... When built [6] ....
'here built (place and State or foreign country) ....
ome port designated ....
wner [7] ....
ddress *(Street, City, State, Zip Code)* [8] ....
ormer owner(s) [9] ....
....

Application (is) (is not) made for award of visual SIGNAL LETTERS. This vessel (is) (is not) equipped with adio-transmitting apparatus.

I CERTIFY that this vessel has not previously been awarded an official number and has never been documented as a essel of the United States under the above or any other name, to the best of my knowledge and belief.

Signature(s) [10] .... Capacity [10] ....

....
(Please type or print name above signature and indicate capacity in which applicant signs.)

) BE COMPLETED BY FORWARDING PORT:

eceived and forwarded
y the PORT OF ....

uilder's certificate as prescribed by 19 CFR 3.12(a)
☐ is ☐ is not on file.

EMARKS [11]

....
(Date) *Documentation Officer.*

TO BE COMPLETED BY HEADQUARTERS:

Official number awarded ....

Visual signal letters awarded ....

....
(Date) *Chief, Merchant Vessel Documentation Div.*

[1] Insert the vessel's name exactly as it will be marked upon the vessel. Show every former name and motorboat number in parentheses.

[2] Give the rig of the vessel as "steam screw," "gas screw," "oil screw," "oil side-wheel," "oil stern-wheel," "schooner," "barge," or some other appropriate description. the vessel is a steam vessel, state whether it is designed to burn oil or coal; if electric drive, whether turbo or oil engine. If the vessel is propelled by sail and machinery. ve the rig as though the vessel were propelled in whole by the engine.

[3] Passenger, freight, tanker, yachting, or some other appropriate description as listed in MERCHANT VESSELS OF THE UNITED STATES.

[4] Give indicated horsepower (IHP) for a reciprocating or beam steam engine, shaft horsepower (SHP) for a turbine, brake horsepower (BHP) for gas or oil engine.

[5] Individual, corporate, or firm name of builder or builders; do not give name of an officer of a corporation.

[6] Give the year of completion of the vessel.

[7] Individual, corporate, or firm name. Do not give name of an officer of a corporation. In the case of ownership by two or more individuals, the name and pro- ortionate interest of each owner shall be shown. If the vessel is owned by the United States of America, so state followed by the words "as represented by" nd the name of the department or agency concerned.

[8] Address at and from which vessel business of the owner is conducted.

[9] The name of every former owner shall be stated. If there was no former owner, that fact shall be stated. If additional space is needed list names on sheet and attach.

[10] In the case of corporate ownership, the application shall be signed in the corporate name by the president, secretary, or a specially authorized officer of the corpora- on or by an authorized agent. In the case of a firm or partnership, the firm or partnership name shall be signed either by a member of the firm or one of the partners, or y a duly authorized agent. In the case of individual ownership by two or more persons, one of the owners may sign his own name as "managing owner" provided there is led with the collector a written authorization for him to act in that capacity signed by the owners of a majority interest in the vessel. The names of all the members of a rm or partnership owning a vessel and the name of each owner of any interest in a vessel shall be given. In every case, the capacity in which the person signs, whether s owner, managing owner, agent, member of a firm, copartner, etc., shall be stated clearly after his signature in the space provided. If an individual executes the applica- on in the name of a corporation, firm, or partnership, the capacity in which the organization name is signed, whether as owner, managing owner, authorized agent, etc., nall be shown immediately after the name of such organization and the capacity in which the individual signs as representative of the organization, whether as president, ecretary, authorized agent, etc., shall be shown immediately following his signature.

[11] Show any previous correspondence or communication with Headquarters covering vessel; circumstances why no builder's certificate filed, etc.

INSTRUCTIONS

Official Number and Net Tonnage.—As a condition to the documentation of a vessel R. S. 4177, as amended; 46 USC 45, requires the official number awarded to a vessel and her net tonnage to be deeply carved or otherwise permanently marked on her main beam; and if at any time she shall cease to be so marked, the vessel shall be liable to a fine of $30 for each omission on every arrival in a port of the United States.

The official number preceded by the abbreviation "No.," and the net tonnage, preceded by the word "NET," must be marked in a conspicuous place on her main beam at the expense of the owner or master, in arabic numerals of block type, as shown below, at least 3 inches in height, when the size of the main beam will permit. If the main beam is of wood, it must be carved or branded in figures not less than three-eighths of an inch in depth. If the main beam is of iron or other metal, the official number and net tonnage must be outlined by punch marks and painted over with oil paint, using a light color on a dark background or a dark color on a light background. The arabic numerals shall be of the following type:

1, 2, 3, 4, 5, 6, 7, 8, 9, 0

The main beam is the beam at the forward end of the largest hatch on the weather deck, which is generally located forward of amidships. In the case of a vessel which does not have a hatch on the weather deck, the main beam is a structural member, integral to the hull.

The official number awarded to a vessel will pertain only to that vessel. If a vessel, having once received an official number, is rebuilt or redocumented, the number originally awarded shall be retained.

IMPORTANT.—The Officer In Charge, Marine Inspection is required by regulation (19 CFR 3.14) to withhold the marine document of a vessel until evidence is furnished to him that the official number has been properly marked thereon. When, therefore, the number has been marked upon your vessel, you should leave notice to that effect at the marine desk in the office of the collector concerned. An inspector will then be sent to examine the vessel, and, if the number is found to be properly marked, he will certify that fact to this office. No fee will be charged for this service. Upon receipt of the inspector's certificate, the official number will be entered upon the vessel's papers, which will then be delivered to you.

Diagram showing how the *signal letters* of the vessel may be communicated to passing vessels.

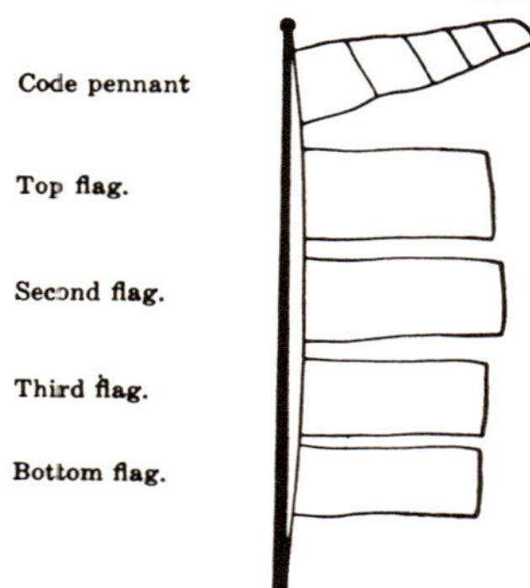

Visual Signal Letters.—All seagoing vessels of 100 tons or over may have signal letters. Signal letters for vessels of less than 100 tons may be awarded upon special application to the Commandant, U. S. Coast Guard If radio call letters are awarded by the Federal Communications Commission, they will be, in general, identical with the visual signal letters. Note the diagram at left showing how the signal letters may be communicated by the international code pennant signaling system to passing vessels at sea or signal stations on shore by the aid of four flags in a signal hoist in one place below the distinguishing code pennant.

Marking of Draft.—The draft of every registered vessel shall be marked upon the stem and sternpost, in English feet or decimeters, in either arabic or roman numerals. The bottom of each numeral indicates the draft to that line. If all the figures indicated in the draft cannot be placed on the sternpost, they may be continued upward on the adjacent part. (Act of Feb. 21, 1891, as amended; 46 U. S. C. 48.)

Marking of Name and Home Port.—The name of every documented vessel (yachts excepted) shall be marked in full upon each bow and upon the stern, and the home port or hailing port shall also be marked in full upon the stern. These names may be painted or gilded or consist of cut, carved, or cast roman letters in a light color on a dark ground, or in a dark color on a light ground, and must be distinctly visible. The letters used shall not be less than 4 inches in height. If any vessel of the United States is found without these names so marked, the owner or owners shall be liable to a penalty of $10 for each name omitted. Every steam vessel of the United States must, in addition, have her name conspicuously placed in distinct, plain letters of not less than 6 inches in height on each outer side of the pilothouse, if it has such, and in case the vessel has side wheels, also on the outer side of each wheelhouse, under the same penalty as provided above. (R. S. 4178, as amended, R. S. 4495; 46 U. S. C. 46, 493.)

On vessels called "double-enders," the letters prescribed by the statute may be placed on the parts corresponding to the bow and stern, and on vessels with sterns not affording sufficient space for letters, they may be placed on the adjacent parts, in both cases so as to conform to the law as closely as possible and so that the hailing port shall be marked at one end of the vessel.

Scows, barges, or other vessels "scow-built" or with square bow may be marked on the bow instead of the side where such marking would be speedily obliterated by chafing against other vessels, spiles, or docks.

The hailing port or port to be marked on the stern may be either the port where the vessel is permanently documented or the place in the same district where the vessel was built or where one or more of the owners reside. (Act of June 26, 1884; 46 U. S. C. 47.)

Documented yachts are required to have their names and hailing ports placed on some conspicuous part of their hulls. (R. S. 4214, as amended; 46 U. S. C. 103.)

GPO 948-663

INDEX